What mattersmost of All

My Calendar is Written in Crayon

SMART ADVICE FROM WORKING SINGLE MOMS

Shirley Jump, Liza Marie Garcia,
and Abby Brundage

NOW SC Press
2017

Copyright © 2017 by NOW SC Press
ISBN 978-0-9987391-0-6

All rights reserved. No part of this publication may be reproduced, distributed, or transmitted in any form or by any means, including photocopying, recording, or other electronic or mechanical methods, without the prior written permission of the publisher, except in the case of brief quotations embodied in critical reviews and certain other noncommercial uses permitted by copyright law.

For permission requests, write to the publisher, addressed "Attention: Permissions Coordinator" via the website below.

1.888.5069.NOW
www.nowscpress.com
@nowscpress

Ordering Information: Quantity sales. Special discounts are available on quantity purchases by corporations, associations, and others. For details, contact the publisher at the address above.

Orders by U.S. trade bookstores and wholesalers. Please contact: NOW SC Press – Tel: (888) 506-9669 or visit www.nowscpress.com.

Printed in the United States of America
First Printing, 2017

Dedications

Shirley Jump: My children are everything to me. Their smiles are a part of all my happiest moments, and their hugs are the best embraces in the world. I am grateful for every moment I have had with them, and thank them for enriching my life in a thousand wonderful ways.

Liza Marie Garcia: I'm dedicating my work on this book entirely to my mother, DiAnne C. Garcia. As we all know, our example of what motherhood looks like begins with our mother and for this I am grateful. My mother was a great example of a selfless mom as I was growing up, taking me to violin and piano lessons, driving me across the Salt Lake valley for dance class and swim team workouts. I pattern the opportunities I provide to my daughters today from all I was exposed to.

As I grew older I learned the stories of her dedication to her children by being willing to work off shifts and take little for herself. I doubt my mother ever lived the concept of "spa day" or a "girls' weekend." My mother is a very talented, artistic woman of action; of these traits the latter is one I coin when speaking of myself quite often. The final dedication of my book and my life is to Him and to Him be all the glory!

Abby Brundage: I am so grateful to the ladies at NOW for bringing me along on this journey! Thank you for allowing me to share a chapter of my story. All of my "mom writings" are dedicated to my boys who have turned my heart into a home; the sun shines brighter and the ice cream tastes sweeter thanks to you! My parents and my support system, you've redefined what family looks like, and it looks beautiful! And to God who has blessed me more than I deserve and brings me to tears with his abundant love, grace and mercy, I treasure the good times, but am forever grateful for the struggles because they have shown me more of You.

Before You Start This Journey...

Wow, has it really been four years since the state of Washington said I was divorced? Such a life changing moment with ups and downs, both personally and professionally, something I think all divorced, single moms can relate to. Despite the challenges and changes, becoming a working, single mom was, without question, the best decision I could have made. My only regret was how much time it took to make my way through the journey.

As one of the co-authors of *What Matters Most of All*, I find myself in that wonderful part of my life where it is all coming together. Doing so "for the good," as they say, something I attribute to hard work and a strong faith.

This book is written from the perspective of three women who are considered thought leaders, business innovators, and experienced mothers. All of us are women trying to live our lives with purpose. In these pages, we offer the lessons that we have learned. Some hard lessons, some bittersweet, but lessons that we realize are common to so many women.

The perspectives in this book are real, all three of us are real, living our lives with children who are looking to us to lead them as they make their way in this world. When we came up with the title, *What Matters Most of All*, we realized it was a very simple answer – we are the kind of women who serve as strong role models to our children. They are watching, learning, and following in our footsteps whether we realize it or not!

We invite you to laugh and cry with us, and for just a moment, know that you are not alone in the struggle to be a successful, working, single mom. The three of us are Strong and Courageous Women – and so are you!

— **Liza Marie Garcia**

Contents

Dedications iii

Before You Start This Journey. v

Chapter One – My Name Tag is Wrong 1

Chapter Two – Sending Out the SOS 15

Chapter Three – The Hair Salon is a Refuge 29

Chapter Four – Sometimes the Tortoise Laps the Hare 43

Chapter Five – I'm Juggling as Fast as I Can 55

Chapter Six – Kids Don't Offer Coffee Breaks ... 67

Chapter Seven – The "Civil" War 81

Chapter Eight – Don't Let the Mess Distract You 91

Chapter Nine – Thank You is More than Good Manners 105

Chapter Ten – What Matters Most of All 117

About the Authors 131

A Day in the Life #DITL 139

Chapter One
My Name Tag is Wrong

Shirley

My name is a funny thing, something I sign on checks, but also a business in and of itself. If I had paused twenty years ago when I started my career, I might have looked ahead and seen the complicated road my name would create. When I sold my first romance novel, my editor asked me what name I wanted to use for my career. Since I was writing romantic comedy at the time, it made sense to keep my married last name – Jump – because it was unusual and a little funny. Sixteen years later, I got divorced.

My identity is now split. There's the professional writer, whose name is still Shirley Jump, because that's the name under which I built a career of more than 60 books. But then there's me, who isn't really her anymore, but if I go back to my maiden name, then that seems weird in work settings.

> I have this confused double identity, one I wanted to shrug off the minute the judge signed the papers ...

Then there's social media. A lot of my readers friended me on my personal Facebook page, which is still under my married name. I debate daily whether to change it to my maiden name and reduce the number of friends to a handful. I have this confused double identity, one I wanted to shrug off the minute the judge signed the papers but will have to wear for the rest of my life, or at least as long as I have books in print.

The whole name thing was weird fallout from divorce that I had never seen coming all those years ago. In the midst of the battle in court, I didn't think about my career or my last name. In the end, like many moms, I kept my married last name legally because I wanted the same last name as my children.

But now that both are adults, that isn't as important, so I go back to the same debate. It is strange to still be signing things with my marital last name. It has sort of, oddly, become a pseudonym because it isn't me anymore.

There was one time when I walked into a bookstore, rounded the corner into the romance section, and saw a woman sitting on the floor reading one of my books. I introduced myself, and she was beside herself, so thrilled to meet an author she loved. I walked out of the bookstore, thinking, *wow, that was a pretty amazing moment*. Then I drove to my son's third grade classroom to serve as room mom. When I walked in the room, no one jumped up from where they were sitting and exclaimed, "It's Shirley Jump, the author!"

Instead, the kids said, "Look, it's Derek's mom!"

I paused. This, I realized, *this* was the true amazing moment. Because at the end of the day, I'm not any particular last name. I'm my kids' mom, and that's a name I'll proudly wear till the end of my life.

Liza

I have always been a strong woman, with a strong voice. I attribute this to my mother, whom I looked at as being strong when I was younger. As I grew taller than her in my teens, I looked at her as being small but mighty, and when I became an adult, I realized the strength it took for her to raise three kids in a difficult time when mom stayed at home and dad worked. I saw her as strong, but in a different way from myself, who juggled a career and family.

I lost that sense of inner strength when I lost my voice and my identity during the three-year battle called my divorce. My entire world changed when I was caught up in the insanely unfair world of family law.

I didn't lose all this in weeks or months, but rather in the years leading up to my divorce. Those years changed me into someone I would never recognize today. When I filed for the divorce, my daughters were only four and five years old. I'm not proud of doing that when they were still so young, and looking back, I see it as a very selfish act but I filed nonetheless, believing it was the right decision at the time.

What caused me to lose my voice? What caused me to lose my identity and my strength? There is no single, neat answer. My knee jerk response blames it on the malicious actions of an overzealous lawyer and vengeful ex-husband to be. To blame it on lawyers and courtroom antics is too easy and not entirely true. Those of you who have gone through a heavily contested divorce, complete with all the trimmings – money, assets, business ownership, children – will understand how a person can get lost and snowed under. I lost my strength during my divorce because at every turn I was battling, defending, fighting.

> The truth is, the real reason I lost my voice during this time was that I wasn't using it.

The truth is, the real reason I lost my voice during this time was that I wasn't using it. Seems simple now, and at the time I probably would have argued there was no way that I – Liza, Business Woman, Business Owner, Super Mom – could ever lose my voice. I was wrong!

I know now that you can lose yourself, lose your voice, and your strength so easily. You can lose it like sand falling away from a sandcastle built on a windy shore, erased little by little until no remnant of any castle exists at all.

I learned many lessons during those difficult years, but one that I share whenever I meet a woman in a similar place. Don't let obstacles derail your focus. For me, I let this incredibly difficult battle of mine completely take my focus away from taking care of myself, being good to myself, being a good mother, and standing strong in who I was at this time of my life. In the end, I lost myself completely.

I learned it all starts inside, in those deep parts of yourself that sometimes get buried or forgotten. It's in those words you speak to yourself. What is your "self-talk"? Do you tell yourself you are strong and capable, or do you tell yourself you feel weak and embattled? How do you keep yourself from being distracted and letting those negative voices in? Do you remember who you are as a person? You are more than just the "mom of …"

Take a moment. Ask yourself those questions. Answer with solid, definitive statements and actions.

For me, I have started operating in a mindful way. When I have to make a vital decision that could change the course of my life, I stop, get quiet, and listen to the Holy Spirit. You can also ask the Holy Spirit to answer any question you have.

Each and every word you say to yourself is important. That inner voice is the first one we hear when we wake up. The internal debate over staying in bed longer, heading to the kitchen for that first cup of coffee, or whether we tell ourselves we are in a good mood or bad mood. Every time we have those thoughts, we are telling ourselves how to feel for the day. We really are. It sets you up for feeling strong, or believing you are weak. It sets the tone for the voice inside you.

What is that voice saying while you are driving the kids to school, or when your mind wanders in traffic? What do you say to yourself when you are being introduced to a new person, when a new opportunity comes your way, or when fear sets in with a new challenge?

I let the negative self-talk win during my divorce instead of listening to the parts of me that knew I was strong, knew I was capable, knew I would do more than survive. I forgot to tell myself that I would come out of this time in my life better than I was before.

For many people, self-talk is in those whispers from God or the Holy Spirit. The positive words that remind you of your worth and strength should be heeded. Too often, women listen to self-talk that is comprised of lies they bought into for many years, so many years that it makes it difficult to distinguish its validity – *you are weak, you are afraid, you are less than.*

Those words are false, and they are the ones that steal your strength and silence your voice.

> I believe any self-talk that is negative, stress-laden, self-doubting, or full of worry is a lie that you are telling yourself.

I believe any self-talk that is negative, stress laden, self-doubting, or full of worry is a lie that you are telling yourself. You are creating the way you look and handle life by believing this lie. Turn those words around and become your own best voice.

The next time you doubt yourself, stop. Question those doubts and ask yourself, why would this statement have any validity? What if what you are doubting about your life, or about yourself, are really just lies, and all those things you s

hied away from are possible? What would happen if you stopped, dug deep…

And told yourself it was possible?

As busy as we are raising kids and dealing with bills and jobs and life, at the end of the day, we come home to our own thoughts and our inner voice. Those things carry us in tough times. Our thoughts become our actions, our actions become who we are, and our strength is either stronger or weaker for it.

I have changed my self-talk and made it a message of empowerment. *I can do this, I am strong, and my voice will never be silenced again.* Do the same for yourself and write the statement that erases your doubts and fears and rebuilds the foundation you lost for a little while. Each day you listen to positive and grateful self-talk makes you stronger. A woman others will look at and see isn't built of sand, but rather of concrete inner strength, standing against any storms that come her way.

Abby

When it comes, it hits you like a ton of bricks.

Bam. You're a divorced, single mom. And boy, is it sneaky. It even got me with a car insurance policy. *Abby Brundage, a divorced woman, will be 37 on …* Thanks for the reminder, State Farm! Your marriage failed, but you're all paid up for the next six months!

You think the day you sign the divorce papers is when the identity crisis starts, but it's not. That is just the day the key goes into the lock that opens the door and welcomes in the parade of surprises that will make you wonder who you are now that you're not the Mrs. you thought you'd always be.

It took me a long time to be able to say the word "ex-husband." Isn't it strange how identifying someone *else* seems to say so much about yourself? Saying I have an ex-husband was like rolling out a banner scribbled with labels for myself. *Inadequate. Disposable. Unattractive. Imperfect.* While the identity I always wanted was sent into a tailspin, there was this new me being involuntarily created.

> I wanted to ignore this new person, whoever she was, but I knew deep down she had potential for greatness.

I wanted to ignore this new person, whoever she was, but I knew deep down she had potential for greatness. I didn't want to know her because to acknowledge her would mean I was accepting this new lot in life. If I could play ostrich and not look at the single mom in the mirror maybe I could convince other people I was better than that. Better than the stereotype I thought summarized the life and appearance of the divorced mother. But while I was avoiding her, I had a glimmer of hope that she was somehow a better version of myself. To unveil her, I still had to navigate some waters of uncertainty.

Last Christmas, I scrolled through Pinterest for ideas to decorate my house – the house I proudly bought on my own to start over with my sons. All the merriment came to a halt when I checked out decorations for the front door. The monogram seemed to be the hot item. A simple wooden letter decorated with bows, polka dots, burlap, or whatever suits your style. I loved the idea until I started thinking about what letter I'd choose. My maiden name? It's not my sons'. My married name? It just doesn't feel like mine anymore, and it hurts too much to claim it. Nothing felt right. The decoration was so insignificant, yet it really spoke to who I was. What is my name now?

But just like the letter on the front door, many of the things that send us spiraling into this identity crisis are on the *outside*. Truth does not stem from external matters. God says that we need to look inside to see what really matters and know who we are.

One day, I took my boys to Magic Kingdom. Our first stop was a photo opp with Mickey Mouse. This was our first family photo with Mickey and first one post divorce. We posed, smiling, the perfect image the photographer wanted. But as we rounded the corner into the gift shop to purchase the photo, I broke down in tears. I had imagined that first Disney family photo for years, but never thought that was how it would look. A single mom holding an eight month old and a toddler. Whose family and life was this?

I tried to hide my face from my boys and put on a smile. My older son, two years old at the time, looked at the photo, then up at me, beaming. "Are we going home now?"

Just as he didn't understand there was so much more left to see in the magical world of Disney, I realized I had been missing the point with my worry about door decorations and family photos. Home to my son was wherever we were. That identity hadn't changed. And neither had mine. I was still myself, still a mom, and still building a home – not the one I had imagined years before – but still a home filled with love, warmth, and memories.

And more importantly, *I* am more than the salutation on the insurance policy, the polka dot letter on the door, or even the family photo with Mickey. I am Mom, and I am able to love my children more deeply than anyone on this earth. These two gifts that God gave me have allowed me to love and be loved in a way that fills my heart on a daily basis.

If you're now checking the "divorced" box you never used to give a second glance to, or juggling a shared custody schedule that was never supposed to be on your calendar, remember the labels the world gives you are not nearly as important as the one God did. You are His child and He entrusted those little ones to you. Remind yourself of that on a daily basis, and you'll find the same key that unlocked a door to an identity crisis can open the door to a new world of sweet, warm memories and unconditional love.

What Matters Most: To Do List

If you are struggling with finding your identity post divorce, try some of these tips:

- Take a sheet of paper and write at the top: "I'm Proud to be ..." and every day add one thing to describe yourself.

- Is there something about your identity as a single mom that you've been avoiding? Something you're ashamed of? Pray or journal about that.

- Schedule a photo session for you and your kids. Create new family photos. If you want, wear Spanx and fake eyelashes. They'll make you feel even more gorgeous than you already are!

- Make a list of the things that set you apart from every other woman. Are you a wonderful singer or great baker? These are the things that people remember about you.

- Support groups can be great for helping you through these new, uncharted waters. Look for one near you to find other single moms who can understand and support you.

Chapter Two
Sending Out the SOS

Shirley

The envelope in my mailbox was small, ordinary, addressed simply to me. I had just moved into my own place at the same time my divorce was finalized, and had my then sixteen-year-old son living with me. I hadn't been smart financially at all before the separation and divorce, and at that time, I was dead broke. I literally had no idea how I was going to fill my empty refrigerator or pay my first city services bill.

Inside the envelope was a check from a friend. Just three hundred dollars, but in that moment, it could have been a million. She had written me a little note about how she made an annual donation of the same amount, but this year, she decided to send it to me. No need to pay me back, she said, just pay it forward someday.

My Calendar is Written in Crayon

> It was such a generous, unselfish thing to do and had come at a critical time.

I sunk to the floor and cried. It was such a generous, unselfish thing to do and had come at a critical time.

For so many years, I had been the one who could do it all. I didn't need help carrying the groceries or getting the kids out the door or managing my career. I had always felt it was weak to ask for help, as if you were admitting you didn't have it all together.

Not having it all together was pretty much my life theme during my divorce. I had knelt down to pray just days earlier, telling God I needed help. I wasn't sure where that help would come from, or how it would appear, but could He please send help? And He did.

By the end of the day, my refrigerator was full and the city services bill had been paid. I stood in my condo, and for a second, felt a flicker of shame that I hadn't been able to do it all by myself. Wonderful friends had carried in the boxes from the moving truck, set up my bookshelves and kitchen, and held me when I cried. Others had brought over flowers or a loaf of banana bread, just something to say, hey, I'm here if you need me.

And today, a friend had sent money with no strings attached.

In the years after my divorce, I struggled financially. I kept wanting to pay it forward, to send three hundred dollars to someone else in need, all the while feeling like I hadn't kept the promise to the woman who sent me the check. Then a friend called, asking me to help her move. I was there the next day with tape and boxes and a willing spirit. Another friend needed help writing something for work, and I spent the afternoon doing that, the two of us huddled over her laptop. A third needed a place to sleep for a couple of nights, and I opened my door.

Paying it forward – helping others – isn't all about money. God wants us to put out our hand to help each other, whether that hand is there to pack a box or make a meal or just hold tight.

If you are feeling lost and wondering where your help is at, take a moment to look for the invisible elves that have been working behind the scenes. The friend who watered your grass on the days you were too emotionally wrought to get out of bed. The neighbor who brought over some cookies on a rainy afternoon. The long distance friend who texted just the right meme when you were struggling.

Then turn around and do the same for those around you. Put a card in the mail to the friend across the country, send a sweet text to that woman who is feeling down, make a dinner for someone who is tired or sick. Do this just as my friend did, with no expectations, no strings. The best way to pay it forward is just do it and watch that helping spirit spread like the incoming tide washing into the empty pockets of sand.

Liza

I was twenty-seven, engaged, and living in Seattle when I started my first company, a technology software firm. Running a fledgling company meant working many hours, employing many people. The business consumed my life.

As my company grew more successful, I could afford to hire assistants, office managers, human resource managers, and all sorts of support staff. It made sense – an efficient, successful business needs an efficient, successful team at its core.

I had two toddlers by the middle of the recession. Around this time, my parents moved to Seattle to be a bigger part of their grandchildren's lives. I'd been married twelve years, and things were already starting to deteriorate in my marriage. I ignored the many signs of what was to come, concentrating on the crazy juggling act of my life.

> ... back then, when I thought I could manage everything, asking for help was a foreign concept.

My world began to turn upside down when the recession hit my business, my marriage fell apart, and my preschool age daughters needed more of me. I should have asked for help; I didn't. Such an obvious thing, but back then, when I thought I could manage everything, asking for help was a foreign concept.

As my life disintegrated, I didn't go to therapy, I didn't go to church. I didn't ask for help in any way from my fellow mom girlfriends. I figured I could handle it. Why not? If I could run a successful multi-million dollar business, why did I need to depend on anyone besides myself?

I was wrong. I look back now and thank God my parents saw my struggles and stepped in, in that unspoken way that parents understand. It was definitely a "God Thing" that my parents lived less than five miles away.

My father and I had long talks. His wisdom and patience taught me more life lessons than he could ever know. He once told me he believed God had called him and my mother to move to Washington state to be there when I needed help picking up the pieces and setting them right again.

When the worry overwhelmed me, my father would assure me that my girls would move through this and be okay on the other side. Even today, I can hear the whispers of my father's sound advice in my head. My father would not only help me by taking on the home tasks vacated by my husband, but my father let me know I wasn't alone and I was stronger than I knew.

The more I learned to ask for help, the more comfortable I got with the concept. Now, it seems so simple – just ask, and help will be there.

I've turned my thinking completely around, and a few years ago, began mentoring women in an active way. Former employees, fellow moms, work friends, and strangers have reached out to me after reading my first business book, seeking me for counsel and advice. I see the fear and worry in their eyes, and I find myself repeating my father's words. *You are strong. You can do this. And I'll be here to help you.*

Isn't that the same message God is giving us every day? Look around you – there are opportunities for you to do the same. The asks might come in the form of Facebook groups, Twitter conversations, or organizations needing volunteers. Reach out, put your hand in theirs, and whisper the words:

You are strong. You can do this. And He is here to help you.

Abby

Has your smoke alarm ever gone off in the middle of the night? You shoot up in bed, use your foggy senses to make sure there is no actual fire, and then begin cursing the batteries. Toss in a sleeping baby, and the level of frustration and panic to replace those cursed batteries gets amplified twenty-fold.

When the writing was on the wall, and I knew my marriage was over, those were the things that panicked me. "What do I do if the smoke alarm batteries die in the middle of the night again? I can't even reach it if I stand on a ladder!" In hindsight, I realize the frivolity of it all, but at the time, those were the worries that churned in my mind. It doesn't take a psychologist to know that anxiety wasn't about the noise or finding the batteries; it was about being alone.

Have you ever spent a day at work, dealing with deadlines, coworkers, and traffic, only to come home to fighting siblings with homework and projects, lunches that need to be packed, and baths that need to be taken? You walk in and realize there is no one else there to hand off the chores to. No one else to sit down with the grumpy seven year old to go over math equations while you make dinner or spend twenty minutes in the bathroom, decompressing. I can't say I've ever *not* survived a night of parenting alone, but there were nights I thought it was touch-and-go.

It's not the big crises that get me down. It's the day in, day out stuff. That five p.m. hour when there's no nap to be had, no bedtime in sight, guilt over screen time has started to settle in, and I'm just worn out from a long day. The little moments can start to weigh heavily, and what should be a drop in the bucket turns into a tidal wave of hopelessness and "Why do I have to do this alone?" If only there were two of me.

Maybe there *can* be two or three or four ...

On 9/11, I was at the gym on my college campus. I remember looking around and seeing people, one at a time, put their weights down and stop moving, focused on listening to the news coming from the stereo system. The clinking, clanging, and chatting quickly turned to silence, then shock. I work in radio, and while I haven't had to break the news of an event like 9/11, in my nine years I have had to open the mic and talk about horrible tragedies like those at Sandy Hook Elementary, Pulse Night Club, and more. In each of these tragedies, once the horror of the event sunk in, the newscasters turned their attention to the moments of hope – the priest who carried injured people out himself, the young teacher who saved her classroom behind a barricaded door, the twenty-something who stood between a stranger and a gunman and risked his life for another's.

In those overwhelming moments, both big and small, the one thing I always come back to is the wise words from the sweater-and-sneaker wearing Fred Rogers. He said, "When I was a boy and I would see scary things in the news, my mother would say to me, 'Look for the helpers. You will always find people who are helping.' "

> Realize that God has put people in your life who can bless you and to whom you can be a blessing in return.

So why not try the same strategy? Restore your hope and look for the helpers. Realize that God has put people in your life who can bless you and to whom you can be a blessing in return.

By letting people help, you are allowing them to be God's instrument. My parents bent over backward to help me after my divorce. At first, I felt terrible I was "burdening" them by moving into their home until I noticed how good it made them feel. My mom got to cook healthy meals for her grandsons and watch them grow. My father got to see the smile on the face of a chubby baby as he "snuck" him a lick of ice cream (I saw every bite, Dad!). When we allow people who are cooperating with God's grace to play a role in our lives, it's a win-win!

If you're hurting right now because you're trying to think of someone in your life who fits the bill but you're coming up short, then step back, take a deep breath, and pray. Ask God to send a helper.

One Sunday God answered a prayer I hadn't even spoken. This particular day was one for the books. I was attempting the impossible, a quiet prayer, kneeling while holding a one year old. He's squirming. I'm sweating. Big brother is asking for goldfish. Next thing I know there's a hand on my shoulder and a woman offering to hold my son. I knew her story. She had done the single-mom-bringing-the-kids-to-church-alone routine, too, several years earlier. As she held him, I just closed my eyes, held back tears and thanked God.

I've found myself doing that quite a bit over the years. When I feel afraid and overwhelmed, I look around, find the helpers, close my eyes, and thank God for these people who have felt the nudge to lend a hand and change three lives for the better. I even found a friend to change the smoke detector batteries. Now, I sleep better at night, not because of the batteries, but because I know I am stronger for doing the one thing I had resisted – asking for help.

What Matters Most: To Do List

When you are struggling with asking for help, try these strategies that have worked for us:

- ✏ Remember that receiving help from others is a way people who love you can show their love.

- ✏ Find a mentor to help you in any part of your life – parenting, career, or spiritual.

- ✏ When you feel overwhelmed, call a friend. Ask for help and offer to cover for her when she needs it.

- ✏ Write a letter to someone who has helped you along the way. Even if it was years ago and the thank you is long overdue, tell them that you appreciate them and will pass the good deed on.

- ✏ Do something small and simple to pay it forward – like paying for a stranger's coffee or offering to pick up their child from school. That way, you feel like you are also doing your part to help. And you never know how much that person might have needed a small miracle to tell them that other people care about them.

Sending Out the SOS

Chapter Three
The Hair Salon is a Refuge

Shirley

Every single time I went to the hair salon, it would rain. Every single, solitary time. I'd spend those couple of blissful, kid-free hours surrounded by the scent of coconut shampoo and floral hairspray, while my hairdresser took me from blah to beautiful. I'd have that moment in the mirror when every strand was in its perfect place, then I'd walk outside, and by the time I got to the car, I looked like I'd been run through a car wash.

I admit, I always felt a little robbed. I wanted to go out dancing or out to dinner, enjoy that perfect hair just a little more. Nine times out of ten, I went straight from the hairdresser to the school parking lot to pick up the kids. Me time was over, and it was back to being Mom.

When the kids were younger, I had to get more creative about finding some "me" time (there are only so many times a year you can go to the hairdresser, after all). For years, I got up an hour or so earlier than the rest of the family. I bought a coffeepot with a timer, so I always had a fresh pot waiting for me. Then I'd take that time to write, read, or just sit outside and enjoy the start of the day. It was quiet, peaceful, and all mine.

My kids are grown up now, but I still get up at a crazy early hour. Sometimes I go straight to a workout, sometimes I just sit outside and listen to the birds. There are nights I take a long walk on the beach, just me and my dog, watching the tide come in and the sun set.

> As my kids have gone from toddlers to adults, I've had to adjust from being a mom to being just me.

As my kids have gone from toddlers to adults, I've had to adjust from being a mom to being just me. At first, it was tough. I didn't have anyone waiting on me to cook dinner or check math answers or drive them to school. That first September after my youngest graduated, I woke up in the morning and got ready to get in the car, and make the morning trek. It took a minute for me to remember those days were over.

It was a bittersweet moment. I suddenly missed having my kids around all the time, missed having my days filled with soccer practices and band recitals and homework lessons. Now I have plenty of "me" time, and most of it has been spent in discovery.

Who am I when I'm not being a mom? Who am I now that I am no longer a wife? I have entirely new dreams and bucket list items. Some I've pursued, some I've left for a later day.

Now I crave kid time – those days when my daughter comes to stay and the three of us are together again, going kayaking or swimming or just hanging out around the kitchen table. I look at my children, these amazing people I am so proud to know, and am grateful I had so many years with them. They are a huge part of what makes me who I am, and now that they are adults, the time we spend together is as precious as those few hours I used to have in the hair salon.

I no longer wish it wouldn't rain on the days I get my hair done. Instead, I wish for sunny days when I have both my children with me. Laughing and talking with those smart, wonderful adults has become the "me" time I had never dreamed would be so fulfilling. And best of all, I don't have to get up way too early to enjoy it.

Liza

I'm writing this chapter while feeling sore from playing tennis this morning. It's only my second morning of exercise this week, and one of not nearly enough times in the last month. No wonder my work clothes are snug and I don't have the energy I used to in the evening. Sometimes I forget that it's important to take time for myself.

When we moms feel great, we exude that spirit to our children, and then they, in turn, feel great because that positive attitude fosters more positivity. The reverse also holds true. When we are stressed out, our children sense it, and that gives them the same stress. These concepts are clear, and something we all know, yet I frequently meet working moms and full-time moms who put themselves at the end of their long To Do list and don't take time for self-care.

> ... our culture makes it seem like taking care of yourself is a selfish act. But it's not – it's critical!

Maybe it's because our culture makes it seem like taking care of yourself is a selfish act. But it's not – it's critical!

I learned this lesson years and years ago when I was a young software engineer, married but no children yet. At the time, I'd secured a very large government account on the west coast. It was one of the largest accounts I had at that stage in my business and since it was early in my career and my business, I hadn't yet assembled the correct team for the support this project required.

So I took on a project by myself that was probably meant for three engineers, two technicians, and a project manager. I thought I could do it all with the help of one assistant because I was Liza – super businesswoman, super technician, and super ambitious.

I killed myself working a hundred hours a week for about two months. From the outside, it looked like everything was under control. The client had no idea that everything was pretty much being held together with a few files, some tape, and a prayer. The database work was in place, but I wasn't.

The project was in its last week, meaning it was pre-testing time, and the last days to finish all the tasks prior to what we called go live day. I had left one of the most complex tasks to finish that week. This task wasn't just the most complex, it was also the most visible. Probably not the best decision I ever made, but I was young and overly confident.

Days before our go live date, a blood vessel burst in one of my eyes, and I started feeling very sick. I later found out I had ear infections in both ears as well. I should have seen the writing on the wall, but I was so exhausted I could barely add one plus one, let alone migrate the entire database.

We did complete the project, however not without help from our vendor and not without the client seeing and understanding what our failings were. I learned a lot of lessons in that moment.

My Calendar is Written in Crayon

> Since that day, I've learned to cut my hours back and to leave breathing room for myself.

Since that day, I've learned to cut my hours back and to leave breathing room for myself. If I had taken better care of myself during that project, I wouldn't have gotten sick so easily, and my stress levels would have been lower. Once I had children, I realized even more how important taking care of myself was. If I wasn't up to snuff, then I wasn't being the best mom for my daughters.

We as moms often try to show the outside world everything is okay. We tell everyone, our children included, that we have it all under control when, in reality, we might be slowly falling apart.

So take a moment to pause, breathe, get your workout in, or even find time for a pedicure. Too much stress causes physical harm, and too little physical exercise creates numerous mental and physical side effects. You need to take care of yourself, so the next time you're stretched to your limits, you will be healthy and strong and able to handle it all like the superwoman you are!

Abby

B.K: Before Kids.

The Hair Salon is a Refuge

Before Kids, there was nothing but time. Well, that and money. I had time to get a pedicure, grocery shop and actually inspect the apples, read a book without pictures, go to the bathroom…. Then my life became infinitely better, but infinitely more crowded. My time wasn't my own once those little lives entered and needed me for every single thing.

When we became moms, we gladly put our needs and our waistlines aside to care for our babies, but as the kids get older and more independent, making ourselves a priority can be confusing and difficult.

In one ear we hear, take time for yourself! In the other, it's stories from moms who say they can't leave their child for more than three hours at a time or they'll start hyperventilating. So let me get this straight. Which of these makes me a lousy mom? The fact that I haven't made it to a hair appointment in eight months or that I have searched online for pre-K boarding schools?

Have you heard the analogy that uses the airplane oxygen mask? During the safety instructions, the flight attendants tell you to place the mask on yourself before assisting others. A passed out passenger is no help to the people sitting around her. So the lesson goes, it's the same for a mom.

My Calendar is Written in Crayon

Care for yourself, and you'll be able to care for your children better.

But what happens when you don't even know where the oxygen mask is? If you're on a flight, the masks drop and you reach for the airsick bag instead, you're in trouble. As single, working moms, it can be tricky to figure out what will provide oxygen that can keep us breathing strong and what is just a temporary breath of stale air. For me, the hair appointments and pedicures are awesome and I savor each one, but if under the surface things are a mess, the perfect color nail polish isn't going to matter.

> I thought I was making myself a priority by "putting myself out there" despite the fact my heart needed time.

I made the mistake of thinking that caring for myself meant dating. I thought I was making myself a priority by "putting myself out there" despite the fact my heart needed time. I was so hurt and confused about my worthiness that I kept fantasizing a new relationship would fill that void. So I reached for the airsick bag in the form of a guy who was completely wrong for me.

Preparing for our date, I shopped for the perfect outfit, thought about all the great conversations we would have, and made sure my lip gloss and hair were perfect. About two hours before we had planned to meet, he still hadn't called to confirm. I texted. He wrote back something about getting tied up with work and maybe needing to cancel. I was so blind and desperate. I offered to drive his direction anyway and asked him to keep me posted.

Meanwhile, I met up with a girlfriend. She probably saw it for what it was and was ready to pick up the pieces when I broke. The date was supposed to start at five. By nine p.m. when I still hadn't heard from him and we were three glasses of wine in, I just looked at her and said, "I've been stood up."

This was my first date after my divorce, and I was stood up for the first time in my life. The next morning I walked out into the kitchen, saw my dad/landlord, and started crying. He told me the guy was a fool.

I was so hurt. But the pain I felt was not just the pain of rejection by this coward, but pain from a reopened, very fresh wound. I made the mistake of thinking I was taking care of myself when I really was allowing someone else to determine my self worth. I was looking for him to heal something that he couldn't heal and fill a void he couldn't fill. In hindsight, and boy, was my sight cleared very quickly, I realized God was stepping in and protecting me from a relationship I was not supposed to be in.

My deep inhale of oxygen came in the form of counseling. Once I was going through the process of divorce and dealing with questions of worthiness and disposability, I knew I had to talk to someone. I sought out a good counselor and made it a priority. I had to make room in the budget and had to impose upon my parents to watch my sons. I knew it was inconvenient for all of us, but I had to take my mental wellbeing seriously if I was going to be the mom my kids needed.

The counseling process was just what I needed. The first session was awkward, but like a good exercise routine builds muscle and endurance, talking to a counselor twice a month brought me to a place of better self-esteem and faith that I could eventually love and trust again.

Because I've found the right way to take care of myself, now when I make time for a pedicure, I have confidence that what's on the inside is even more beautiful than the perfect shade of pink on my toes.

What Matters Most: To Do List

If you are having a tough time carving out time for yourself, then try some of these options:

- If you think you might be reaching for the wrong way to relieve stress or reward yourself for hard work – bad habits like drugs, excessive alcohol, or unhealthy relationships – consider replacing that with something healthier, like a physical activity you enjoy, time with friends, or getting active in a church community.

- Have you considered seeing a counselor? Even if you are years past your divorce, it can do a world of wonders.

- Enlist a friend to keep you accountable for regular walks or a monthly pedicure. Going together gives you both a momentary escape.

- Pre-book your hair appointments! When you leave the salon, set the next appointment right then and there.

- If you are stressed in your life, remember you are bringing physical and mental harm to yourself. Find an outlet to relieve this stress.

- Remember it's contagious – when you feel great, you are a more positive mother and your children feel that energy!

The Hair Salon is a Refuge

Chapter Four
Sometimes the Tortoise Laps the Hare

Shirley

When I was pregnant with my first child, one of my mom's friends sat me down and told me that motherhood was a marathon. She explained that being a mom is a long, hard journey, and a lot of the time, you can't see what is around the corner, have no idea what to expect at the next mile marker. You will have times when you feel strong, times when you feel weak, and times when you feel you can't go another step. But in the end, you will move forward because your children are counting on you.

I got a strong dose of that when I had my second child. My son barely slept and ate every two hours, all day long. I was so exhausted at the end of the day I'd fall asleep the second I put him to bed. Those early years are still a blur, when my main focus was just trying to get through the day.

About seven years ago, I started running. To relieve stress, lose a few pounds, and get out of the house. I started running short distances, then worked my way up to a half marathon and later a half Ironman triathlon. Those races were much like motherhood – hard and arduous and long. There were many times I wanted to quit, hundreds of times I'd round a corner and see a hill or a long, flat stretch that seemed to go on forever and think I couldn't run another step.

In the beginning, I did quit a lot. I'd walk, then be mad at myself, then try to run again, and end up walking, feeling defeated and tired. On one run filled with some especially tough hills, I thought back to those days with my son when it seemed like I was never going to get more than a couple hours of sleep, when I felt like all I wanted to do was quit.

But I couldn't. There was this living, breathing human being counting on me, his little hand curled around my finger, his eyes filled with trust that I would be there, every single hour of every single day, to feed him, protect him, and love him. When I

> When I wanted to quit my mom job, I'd remind myself that I was strong, I could do this, and that someday, it would all get easier.

My Calendar is Written in Crayon

wanted to quit my mom job, I'd remind myself that I was strong, I could do this, and that someday, it would all get easier.

I looked at the hill before me now and realized I was strong. That I could conquer this hill, and once I reached the top, it would get easier. Every step was difficult, painful, and my lungs were screaming, begging for a walk break. But I kept on running, repeating over and over again in my head, *I am stronger than this hill. I am stronger than this hill.*

It has become a mantra for the tough moments in my life, through my divorce, my days of starting over, the financial and child challenges I've faced. *I am stronger than this problem. I am stronger than this worry. I am stronger than this moment.*

That, I think, is what mom was trying to tell me so many years ago. In a marathon, you have to dig deep to find your strong. You have to believe in yourself when everything in your body is saying otherwise. And you have to hold tight to the thought that you are strong. Stronger than any challenge that comes your way.

Then you put one foot in front of the other and keep on climbing. I promise, you will eventually crest that hill, and as you look down, you will see the easy, paved road ahead that you worked so hard to reach.

Liza

Anyone who has ever run a race probably knows the tremendous rush that fills you when you see the finish line. That was my favorite part of running races, from 5Ks to a full marathon. Once I caught a glimpse of the finish line, I would step up the pace, proud I had been able to hold back a little energy for that last final burst. I'd secretly be singing the theme song from "Rocky" in my head as I passed people and finished strong.

The finish line is a huge deal to me. When I started training for triathlons, I was thrilled to be able to pass three finish lines for each section of the race – swim, bike, and run. As a single working mom, that journey is harder because the finish line is often so far out you can't see it.

During those challenging years, I would keep in mind the saying, *it's not a sprint, and it's a marathon.* After running my first full marathon in 2011, I saw this in a literal sense. That year was the year I filed for separation and divorce, and it was also the year I started running.

How did I run the Las Vegas marathon, all 26.2 miles, without walking or without stopping when I ran my first mile just eleven months earlier? Sort of the same way you become a parent. You give birth, something you never did before that day, then are thrown headfirst into raising that child into a functioning little human.

You approach both with a little training. When I first started running, I found this great training guide on the Internet that showed you how to train to run a half marathon. The first week, I'd run a mile on Mondays, a mile and a half on Wednesdays and so on and so forth. The schedule built gradually until one day, you're running ten miles in a single afternoon. You learn so much about your strength, both inner and outer. And most of all, you learn if you start out small and gradual, you can build on that until you reach a point you may have thought unreachable at first.

I remember the day I ran twenty miles for the first time. I was so completely astonished that I cried, so proud of myself and so awestruck, especially when

I thought back to how it all started with that first mile.

Parenting also starts with that first mile. That first year with your newborn is like a baby boot camp. You know what I mean – all the sleep deprivation, constant worries, and frequent questions. Although there are hundreds of books full of wisdom, nothing on paper really prepares you for that real life experience. I remember wishing I had an undergrad degree in elementary education when my daughters were young because my business degree was better preparation for a workplace than those challenging days.

> With any new job, the longer you are there, the more confident in your decisions...

With any new job, the longer you are there, the more settled you are in year two than in year five. You gain confidence in your decisions and familiarity with the environment – the same thing that happens as you make your way from one year to the next with your children.

Even though the finish line of the mother marathon is about twenty-one years in the making, remember that each year you parent, you are working your way through life's challenges and changes. There will be tough moments, easy moments, and moments that will make you cry, but if you remember parenting is all about the marathon and not the sprint, you'll be able to take the time to enjoy that incredible journey.

Abby

If one more person told me "This won't last forever," I was going to scream.

My first baby had a mild case of colic, I had a mild case of postpartum depression, and my husband had a very demanding job. Put it all together, and I had a rough couple of months where no advice from the outside made anything better. But that particular phrase was especially bothersome to me.

It didn't matter that in a few months I was going to get more sleep. I needed sleep now. I found no solace knowing the baby would eventually stop crying. I wanted a cooing baby in my arms right then. I believed my friends when they said there were bright skies ahead, but the dark clouds of the present were making the days long and trying. One night after a long day of crying from both the baby and me, my husband asked what I wanted for dinner. I just rested my head on the back of the couch, held back tears, and said, "I just don't want tomorrow to come." He suggested we order a pizza.

Still, I hung on to the words with hope, knowing that the trials of this phase were not going to last forever. I had to take it one day at a time, sometimes one half hour at a time. Like running a long race, some miles are grueling and make you want to quit, and some are right when you hit your stride and get that runner's high. Taking it one mile at a time gets you to the finish line.

I also find myself saying "This won't last forever" during some of the most cherished moments. Like when we all snuggle in bed together, when they reach up and grab my hand, or ask me to marry them. I kiss the cheek of my younger son in all its chubbiness and just breathe him in. Sometimes he will come back for another and just press his cheek into my lips. I know that in a few years the chub will be gone and he will turn away from my affection. So for now, I watch them and think, "It's not forever that we will be in this place. They will be grown before I know it."

It's funny how those four words "This won't last forever" hold two meanings. It's both a hope in the promise of things to get easier in the near future and a sad realization the moment will soon be gone and we'll be left looking back.

But this phase — this challenging one of being a working single mom, working full time — we definitely want it to pass, right?

But what if God wants *this* moment to be the one where He works mightily through us? What if in this moment, He wants to turn us into the strong, faithful woman He has always known we could be? What if this mile, where the run is the most difficult, is the one where we find out what we are really made of?

If you handed me the keys to a time machine and given me the opportunity to leap forward out of the fire of divorce, I would've gladly taken them and offered to leave the machine gassed up for the next girl. But in that time I discovered things about myself that were buried and just needed a chance to come to the surface. I found I could be forgiving, humble, and faithful. I also saw I needed to work on boundaries, my temper, and appreciating the people who love me. If I had sprinted through that phase, what lessons would I have missed?

The days of single parenting might be filled with challenges and places we don't want to be, but they are a gift, and they won't last forever. What a shame it would be to look back and realize you always wanted tomorrow. That might just leave you longing for yesterday.

What Matters Most: To Do List

Are you feeling like the marathon of motherhood is too hard to conquer? Try some of the below tips and know you aren't on that journey alone.

- If you're going through a difficult time, think back to another trial and write about it. Write what you were afraid of, how you handled the situation, and what the outcome was. Realize you survived it, one day at a time.

- Set a time in the middle of the day to stop and take deep breaths, say a prayer, walk the stairs in your office. Use this time to refocus so you can walk through the rest of the day with strength and confidence!

- Don't be so hard on yourself if you feel like you aren't giving it your all. Motherhood is not a competition, and your kids are going to be just fine even if every moment isn't perfect.

- Take time to recharge with other mom friends. Sometimes all you need is a walk break to gather your energy for the next challenge.

Chapter Five

I'm Juggling as Fast as I Can

Shirley

I have worked at home since my first child was born. I have almost always been a writer, so the transition to work at home mom was relatively stress free, especially since my firstborn, my daughter, was a pretty easy baby. She was one of those kids who took to naps, who slept through the night at four weeks old, who was just as happy going on a walk as she was playing with toys. I set up a nice little schedule around her naps and bedtime and was almost as productive post baby as I had been before baby. I had a thousand wonderful moments with just me and my daughter because I was there with her, all day, every day.

When my daughter was almost five, I gave birth to my son. From the minute he was born, he was a handful. Naps were such a battle, I gave up on them fairly quickly. Bedtime was also a constant war, and there were many, many nights I was up till one or two in the morning, rocking him or pacing, crying as much as him, I think, and begging him to please sleep. During the day, he was a busy, curious, and determined kid, always into something that he shouldn't be.

My work schedule fell apart. I was exhausted all the time, and I missed deadlines. I reduced my workload, which reduced my income, and created a vicious circle. It was tough – I'm not going to lie. There were days when I wished I had a job outside the house so I could get away and actually get something done.

Things eased up when they were both in school, of course, and I began to find my rhythm as a mom and as a writer. After my divorce, I was the sole financial provider for myself and my son. That was a terrifying thought. My income fluctuates, my paydays are never regular, and every single check depends on me and whether I am productive that week or not. No work equals no money. I don't get sick days or personal days or paid vacation days because I'm the whole company. Just me.

There are days when the pressure is overwhelming, when I once again think about how a regular job would make life so much easier. More predictable.

But then I look at the last couple of years, and the impromptu lunches I've gone to with my son (who still lives with me) or the quiet conversations we have at the end of his day, and I realize that God blessed me richly with the ability to work at home.

> I saw him sitting there on the sofa and felt a wave of gratitude that my job has blessed me with time with him.

The other day, my son came home from work, hungry and tired. I made him a snack, then brought it to him in the living room. It wasn't quite five, and I had turned off my computer just minutes before he came home. I saw him sitting there on the sofa and felt a wave of gratitude that my job has blessed me with time with him. Time he didn't get when he was little because he was the second child, and I was so sleep deprived I could barely function.

"Do you realize," I said as I handed him a peanut butter and jelly sandwich, "that when you were little, you and I never really got to spend time together, just the two of us? But now, it's become just you and me, and we get to hang out a lot."

He's a teenager (although he'll tell you he's an adult), and although we are close, there are less and less of those moments when he opens up to me, so I wasn't quite sure how he'd respond.

"Yeah, Mom, I noticed," he said, and in his eyes, so like my own, I saw a spark of happiness. Then he patted the place beside him and grabbed the remote. "Want to watch a movie with me?"

Liza

I've always been a full-time working mom. For that matter, I've always worked full time, from the day I graduated from college. In the first few years of my marriage, I started working for myself in my own software tech company that had offices in Portland and Seattle with clients across the United States. I spent most of the first ten years of my marriage on planes, trains, and automobiles, working many, many hours to get my startup off the ground.

Although my husband at the time and I knew we wanted a family, neither one of us was in a big hurry to begin having babies. It wasn't until we had been married for seven years that we decided we would start trying.

I always said and felt that I would quit my job when I became a mom. At the time, I had pretty negative feelings about women who employed nannies. I believed that to really be a mom, you had to be a full-time mom. But as I went through visits with an infertility specialist, I realized I was in no position to sell off my company to become a mom.

My ex-husband never worked outside the home, and I was the sole and complete financial support for my entire marriage. My technology company provided all we could want financially for nearly our entire marriage, which meant it wasn't financially feasible to sell it off or to quit. So I employed a full-time nanny for about four and a half years and then switched to part time help for the next three years to help me care for my girls.

Having a nanny wasn't my first choice, but it was a choice that benefited my family, and fortunately for us, my daughters' first nanny was an amazing, young teacher who loved my daughters as if they were her own. Hiring someone allowed me to be more present at work, and more present in the hours I spent with my children. But there were still a few tradeoffs.

When we had playdates while my daughters were young, I would sometimes block out my schedule to attend, and sometimes my nanny would attend in my place. When things at work were especially demanding, the other moms would sometimes see my nanny more than me. Hiring help after we started having children was our choice to keep the business going. I met many mothers who judged that decision and my choice to work full time.

> I wanted my girls to see that I was a smart, dedicated mom who also cared about her career ambition.

I wanted my girls to see that I was a smart, dedicated mom who also cared about her career ambition. I might not have been there for every recital or school athletic game, but I was there for every moment that mattered. And because I didn't have all those pressures solely on my shoulders, I was able to enjoy the time I did have with them much more. In fact, it is safe to say I was very deliberate about my time with my girls, which also meant I was more present with them.

For those of you who struggle with making the right decisions about working and childcare, I hope you realize that there is no right or wrong choice. There is only the one that works best for your family. If you are a more present, engaged mom because you chose to go in one direction or the other, that's truly all that matters. In the end, it's about keeping your children fed, clothed, and most of all, happy.

Abby

Confession: I was dying to go back to work after my first son was born.

The mom who says she pulled out of the driveway sobbing at the end of her maternity leave was not who I saw in the mirror that day. Of course I missed my baby, but to be back at work, feeling like a human being who was needed for more than a milk supply or a clean diaper, made me feel like myself again.

That's not to say I don't fight a constant battle between guilt and time. I love my job and I love my children, but to find the balance where I feel like I'm giving enough to both is nearly impossible.

The question I get most often about my job as a morning radio host is: What time do you get to work? I always answer that question with embarrassment. 5:35 a.m. I crack the mic at six a.m. and I only get to work 25 minutes prior to that. Meanwhile, other morning show hosts arrive at four a.m., 4:30 maybe. I feel unprofessional admitting that I don't spend two hours getting everything in its place before the show starts.

The flip side of that coin is that every morning at five a.m., I meet my sitter in the driveway so I can leave my sleeping children behind in their beds and head to work. I don't get to see their messy heads of hair and sleepy eyes in the morning or kiss them as they start their school day. I don't know if the sniffles I sent them to bed with the night before are cleared up or if they should stay home from school to get better.

> It's the battle every working mom fights, and the single, working mom fights it on a level that is gladiator-worthy because she doesn't have a second parent at home to help fill the gaps.

Every time I pull away, I feel like I don't give enough at work and I don't give enough at home. I know I'm not the only one who wrestles with these feelings. It's the battle every working mom fights, and the single, working mom fights it on a level that is gladiator-worthy because she doesn't have a second parent at home to help fill the gaps.

Each time the field trip permission slip comes home, the single, working mom checks her calendar to see if maybe *this time* she can chaperone. Meanwhile she fights back the feelings of jealousy toward the mom who is at every school function and field trip. When she does request time off to be there for the Mom & Me Breakfast or an open house, there's that twinge of worry that work might hold it against her and give that vital promotion to someone else who is "more dedicated."

How do we find a place of peace? A place where we are comfortable with what we give our children and confident we are putting in our fair share of effort at work? I'm not sure it's fully attainable, but we might get close to that place with good communication.

In the evening when I have to sit in front of the computer for thirty minutes, I tell my kids, "I just have to get this done, and then I'm all yours. I wish I could get all my work finished at the office, but I can't. I would rather be building a train with you, and I am so grateful that you are being patient." Then I stick to my word and put the computer away after those thirty minutes have passed. I'm not saying I am perfect at this, but I am trying. And then the nights when I don't have any work to bring home, I try hard to give them all of me. I have set an alarm on my phone, and every day at four p.m., the words *Turn me off* pop up on the screen.

We need to speak to our bosses and coworkers in the same way. Maybe your boss isn't waiting to build a train with you, but sometimes you might have to put work on the backburner so the kids know they are your top priority. As my older son's first day of preschool approached, I asked my boss for the morning off so I could walk my son to his classroom. His reply? "It's not the first day of kindergarten, just preschool." My boss's children are grown so this phase of parenting is long behind him, and he managed the early years with kids differently than I do. I understood his response but explained that my son had never been out of the house for care. This was the first time he would be with a teacher, other kids, and in a classroom environment. Maybe this wasn't his first day of kindergarten, but this was his *first* first day, so it was a big deal for us. I promised that once I was done with drop off I'd be at work and giving it 100%.

Both of these situations are pretty pie in the sky. It's not always like this. Sometimes we give too much in the office and hurt our children, and other times we build the train and miss a deadline at work. What matters most is that we accept the fact that we are giving it our best shot, give ourselves a little room to be imperfect, and realize that 5:35 a.m. is still pretty darn early.

What Matters Most: To Do List

If work has you feeling overwhelmed, take a cue from some of these suggestions. Hopefully they will help you find a little more balance:

- Be sure to carve out time for your kids, even if you are in the middle of a project or have a giant To Do list. Even fifteen minutes can make a difference for your child.

- If you are fortunate enough to have a good relationship with your boss, discuss a better work life balance. Be open to new ideas.

- Next time you have to work at home during family time, take a moment to talk to your child about what you are working on. Could they help?

- If you work at home, be sure to set regular work hours so that you don't feel as overwhelmed and can have family time, too.

✏️ Stop comparing yourself to other moms. No one has it all together.

Chapter Six
Kids Don't Offer Coffee Breaks

Shirley

Years ago, in the days before I carried a cell phone everywhere, I was always running late. I remember when my fancy digital watch, with an alarm and two built-in time zones, started losing twenty minutes a day. I'd made three trips to the store that week and, every time, forgot to buy a new battery. A mom on a constant schedule, I needed an accurate timepiece, so I grabbed the only other watch I own, a delicate silver one my grandmother left me when she died.

Nana's watch is small, with a diamond encircled face and a sliver of a band. It's beautiful and petite, just like she was. I've always loved it, but rarely wear it. It's the old fashioned, battery free kind that needs winding each night. For me, a person who has trouble remembering to feed the cats, wearing a watch requiring any degree of upkeep is a bad idea.

The first few days I wore Nana's watch, I kept forgetting to wind it and still ended up late for everything. But by week's end, its elfin face and ticking second hand were as familiar to me as the feel of Nana's hand in mine when I was a child.

Wearing the watch wrapped me in memories of Nana. She used to take regular walks around the yard, just to see the loganberry trees in bloom. After dinner, she and Grandpa would walk me down to the 7/11 for a packet of M&Ms. We spent countless afternoons strolling downtown, window shopping and dreaming of things to buy and adventures we'd have someday.

Nana appreciated the value of time. Her son, Bobby, died when he was eight in a tragic accident that left a measure of perpetual sadness reflected in Nana's eyes. In 1976, Nana herself slipped through Death's grasp when she had a brain tumor removed successfully. We celebrated the bicentennial of our country that year, cheering for the woman who was still here to sing silly songs and give advice on making potato salad.

Nana refused to waste a second of the extra time granted to her. She taught me piano, asked about every school day, and waded with me through boxes

www.nowscpress.com/crayon

of photographs and memories, trying to imprint legacies on an eleven-year-old girl who couldn't know then that time would ever feel short.

She laughed, she cried, she hugged, she kissed. She lived.

> In the busyness of my life with two kids, a cat, a dog, a job, and a home, I often forgot to slow down and really see the little things around me.

Years later, when she passed away, Nana left me the watch. In the busyness of my life with two kids, a cat, a dog, a job, and a home, I often forgot to slow down and really see the little things around me. Bread was store bought, self-scrubbing bubbles cleaned bathrooms, and my car was a mobile office between soccer games and Brownie troop meetings.

When Nana's watch stopped one day because I'd forgotten to wind it again, I was lost. The children and I were shopping, on our way to an appointment that seemed important at the time.

I stopped in the middle of the store and looked around for a clock, muttering to myself, annoyed. The children started whining about missing some show on TV. Sensing an opportunity, my son darted across the aisle to a toy and my daughter headed for some books nearby. I had melting ice cream in the cart, cranky kids, and someplace I had to be. I didn't need another frustration.

I tapped the watch with the futile hope that it would magically start again. When I did, I had a flash of memory. Nana, my mother, and I were strolling in the sunshine at a sidewalk sale. We bought a book for a dime, a drink from the soda fountain, and nothing else. Twenty five years later, I still remember it as one of the best days of my life because every moment seemed to last forever.

I realized I'd been letting schedules and errands swallow those mini-moments in my own life, ruled by the ticking of a clock that weighed heavy on my shoulders. I abandoned the cart and joined my kids, bending down to see the toys at their level. I marveled at the latest Buzz Lightyear and a colorful new Harry Potter book cover. Hand in hand, the kids and I ambled through the aisles, poking at this toy, pushing the buttons on that one, dreaming of Santa and birthdays and days to come. We wandered by the pet department, made friends with a hamster, and chatted with a parrot.

My Calendar is Written in Crayon

We arrived home much later, carrying a puddle of ice cream in the grocery bag, and one new goldfish. I'd missed my appointment, but it didn't matter. After dinner, we explored our neighborhood on foot, hunting for squirrels and rabbits in the summer evening light. We fed the ducks at the pond, soared through the air on swings and played a rousing game of tag. When we returned home, we were exhausted but laughing. And we all had another happy memory to hang onto.

That night, while I turned the tiny knob to wind Nana's watch, I realized why my grandmother had left me this particular piece of jewelry. Her legacy wasn't a million dollar home on a hill or a priceless art collection. Her gift was much simpler, one we often forget in our calendar-driven lives. She gave me the gift of time, wrapped up in a watch that needs daily attention, a continuous reminder that our days pass as fast as summer storms.

In its tiny silver face, I see Nana, and in the ticking of its second hand, I hear the running journey of my life. That's when I turn off the phone, close the calendar, and take the kids outside to greet the first daffodils of spring.

Liza

I am a "routine" person. For many of us, that commitment to a routine develops when we have our first child. And while I did have more challenges as a new mom because I was working as an active CEO in my tech company, I have pretty much always been committed to a schedule.

Even when I was young, I loved routines and organization. I remember being co-head cheerleader my sophomore year in high school and wanting to organize and take conference notes during our meetings. How I even knew what conference notes were amazes me to this day.

> I feel like a ship crossing a vast ocean, confident it will reach its destination because it's following a firm navigational plan.

Routine helps me move through my life with certainty and, in a weird way, it helps me feel good about my life's direction. I feel like a ship crossing a vast ocean, confident it will reach its destination because it's following a firm navigational plan. This in turn helps me with raising my daughters. I believe it helps my children as well because they can count on routine occurrences.

When my daughters were young, we had a daily theme. Mondays were Play-Doh Day, Tuesdays were Dance Day, Wednesdays were Craft Day, and Thursdays were Dress-Up Day, and so on. My girls were in preschool then, and they woke up each morning, excited for that day's theme activity.

Also during those years, my girls had a specific bath, nap, eating, and bedtime routine. Now that they are preteens with busy school and sport schedules, the bedtime routine is the only one of these routines still in place. The others have yielded to reading, instrument practice, and athletic routines.

I believe children like order. Routines and organization provide a dependable, stable base, yet also allow children to find the space they need to make their own choices outside of their schedules, which helps them navigate this always changing and vast world they live in.

The statistics are there to back this up; dozens of studies have found that when children have standard bedtime routines, they do better in school. Other studies have shown that for children living in chaos, sometimes a simple routine might be the only thing that child can count on.

I miss the dress-up days and craft days, but I also really enjoy the time we spend now, running from one activity to the next, then coming back home to settle in with pajamas and tooth brushing and one last goodnight. My children have learned to count on these routines, but so have I.

I love knowing the end of my day will be spent with the two people who matter most to me in the world. I hope as they grow older, they know the one routine they can always count on is the way I love them.

Abby

I come from a German-Catholic family from the Midwest. Between the brats and kraut, Sunday Mass, Holy Days, and Packer games (which sometimes get treated as holy days), growing up my life was filled with tradition. Just like football players tapping the school mascot logo on the tunnel wall before they run out onto the field, having family traditions gives us a sense of belonging to a team. Some of my family's traditions were normal; we ate breakfast together every day, regardless of our school schedules. Some were bizarre; we eat reheated Taco Bell tacos on Christmas morning. To this day, my dad goes out on Christmas Eve, gets an assortment of tacos, all the fixings on the side, and then reheats them in the oven on Christmas morning. It's been our thing for about 18 years now. We laugh and make the same jokes every 365 days. Tradition!

Between the holidays and the dinner table, you probably have some traditions in mind that you wanted to start or continue with your family. Divorce has a way of confusing us when it comes to carrying on these special moments. A Christmas or birthday morning tradition doesn't feel as special when it's only done every other year.

One of my favorite holiday traditions is cozying up on the couch with a cup of coffee or hot cider and watching the Macy's Thanksgiving Day Parade. My mom and I watched it every year as we sliced carrots, basted the turkey, and sprinkled the dried onions on top of the green bean casserole. We would stop everything to see the Radio City Rockettes' famous kick line. Now because of our shared time, my children are always away on Thanksgiving morning. I text their dad to ask if they saw the Snoopy balloon in the sky, the Sesame Street float roll by, or the big guy in red closing out the parade. The tradition that I held dear wasn't going to look the same in my little family, and now every Thanksgiving is met with a bit of sadness.

> ... sometimes the moments we think are going to be magical are simply ho-hum, and the ones we expect to be uneventful can be the most memorable.

But one thing I've come to learn is sometimes the moments we think are going to be magical are simply ho-hum, and the ones we expect to be uneventful can be the most memorable. So my efforts are now focused on the every day. One small thing we do at the dinner table is ask, "What was your favorite part of the day?" It's simple. Most nights my three year old says, "Right now!" My heart melts and I feel like saying, "Me too, thanks to that answer," but instead I try to come up with an original. This simple ritual has become something that makes our dinner time and family special. They even remember to bring the question up when we are out to dinner, and we bring a little bit of home to the outside world.

These routines and traditions are sources of comfort, even for adults. When the time change happens and the sun is in a different spot in the sky during our commute, it makes us feel out of whack for a while. Our kids thrive on routine. All the parenting books told us how important it is, and we bought into it, agreeing with every word. Then, divorce happened, and any semblance of a routine became a thing of the past. Bedtime is always at eight. Then thanks to your divorce, every few days that's out the window! Every Saturday afternoon everyone chips in to do yard work. Now that raking has to wait for every other Saturday.

But this is reality, and we're making the best of it, so get unconventional with routine by not setting it by day or time, but by activity. When we are in the car together and getting close to home, my guys start looking for checkpoints. I call out landmarks and they say "Check!" as soon as they see it. It's a good way to get them familiar with the neighborhood, but it also gives us a small routine for most every drive home.

Don't wait for the important days to do important things with your kids. Look for the opportunity for family traditions in the every day. Then every day can feel like Christmas. Minus the reheated taco.

What Matters Most: To Do List

Is your schedule making you crazy? Or are you having trouble setting one and committing to it? Try these tips to make life a little easier.

- To build in some kid-connection time, come up with a question you can ask consistently at the same time each day – the drive to or from school, at bedtime or at the table during a meal.

- Allow for flexibility. Sometimes dinner will come from a drive-through, giving you and the kids a little extra time on the playground or one more round of Pictionary.

- If things feel out of control, try adding in more routines. That may help you move through your life with more ease and help create the consistency your children crave.

- Create fun "theme" days, especially with younger children. It gives them a fun routine to look forward to.

- Pick a day on the calendar and make it your family holiday. Celebrate together with a

My Calendar is Written in Crayon

silly breakfast, a game night, or even a cake with candles.

Chapter Seven
The "Civil" War

Shirley

Getting divorced is like taking all your emotions, stuffing them into a bag, jumbling them all together, then dumping them back into your heart and mind. I have felt love, I have felt hate, I have felt bitterness, and I have felt forgiveness.

It is so much easier to let the anger and bitterness win. To grumble and complain and point the finger at your ex. I have done that, more times than I like to admit, but in the last year, I have worked very hard at doing the opposite.

Last year, I went through a lot of personal problems that made me really sit back and reevaluate my life and how I was handling things. I started making a list of things I wanted to change, and on that list, I wrote, *choose compassion over anger, grace over judgment.*

The second I wrote those words, my ex texted me. Things between us had been rocky, to say the least, and I dreaded reading the text. Turns out he'd been in a bike accident and wasn't injured that badly, but was worried nevertheless about his injuries. I took a deep breath and thought back to what I had just written. *Choose compassion over anger, grace over judgment.*

I texted back, with sympathy and worry, offering some advice and most of all, compassion. It was a great conversation, one with no bitterness or anger, and I think both of us felt better at the end of it.

I remember when my mom was sick, and I was running back and forth between her house and the hospital. Every day, I battled the Boston commuter traffic, grumbling about the drivers who cut me off, the seemingly endless red lights. I felt my stress level rising with every mile.

> ... maybe those moments are when God wants you to pause and have compassion. We never know what other people are battling.

Then I paused and remembered something someone (I forget who) had once said to me about things like that: maybe those moments are when God wants you to pause and have compassion. We never know what other people are battling. That guy who cut me off may be rushing to get to the bedside of a sick relative.

Or the woman who dawdled at the red light might be crying over the loss of a job. And maybe the delay was meant to save me from an accident. God has a plan in place at all times, and learning to relax into that makes life far less stressful.

It's the same in dealing with my ex. We don't talk every day anymore, so I have no idea what stresses he is dealing with or what might have upset him when we have a less than civil exchange. I'm trying in those moments to take a breath and remember that God wants me to pause and have compassion. He wants me to fight less, understand more, and set an example for my children. I wrote those words on a card and taped them over my bathroom mirror, so I remember every single day to *choose compassion over anger, grace over judgment.*

Liza

The concept of making peace with my ex is a really difficult one for me, and I'm certain it will be written with the least amount of words of all the chapters.

Although I've now been divorced since 2012, the court motions, court trials, mediations, arbitrations, verbal disagreements, and the legal conflicts against me are still a part of my life. And of course the billing from my family law lawyer has not yet ceased.

So I know a little about feeling like it would be "nearly" impossible for me to love or pray for the father of my daughters even after this much time has passed. Notice I said "nearly."

For me, learning to do that started with saying "no" to the continued conflict. I don't want to stress and live my life under the microscope of my ex-husband and the family law legal system. I have also worked hard on my end to say "no" to a conflict-filled relationship with my ex-husband.

Saying all this doesn't necessarily mean all the conflicts are handled or have disappeared. It simply means I have found a new way to handle it using prayer. I have learned there is a benefit to praying that my ex-husband finds a new life, a new relationship, a new interest to help him move forward. I don't wish ill will on anyone, and I want my daughters to look at their father and see that he is happy and secure. I'm certain they have been aware of the tension between us, and I'd like them to see more peaceful days going forward.

The "Civil" War

> Prayer for him will benefit my daughters and is also necessary to benefit their well-being. Knowing this makes it easier to say those prayers, and to say them with an open heart.

Without question, I wish my daughters had a wonderful father or even a father that had their best interests in mind. In my case, it is difficult to concede my ex-husband is, at minimum, a decent human being, so certainly the "loving him" part is completely unfathomable. However, I don't hate him. Prayer for him will benefit my daughters and is also necessary to benefit their well-being. Knowing this makes it easier to say those prayers, and to say them with an open heart.

Abby

You've probably heard statistics about children of divorce. Something like they are more likely to abuse drugs, leave the church, join the circus, grow a third ear .... Just pick something that will make you feel rotten, and that's what your divorce is doing to your child.

When my divorce was finalized, my sons were eleven months and two years old. I just kept thinking that in these formative years, they need to be around a mom and a dad. They are like little sponges, just soaking up the world around them. Other people found it comforting to tell me it's better they aren't older so maybe they won't remember. I don't think it matters their age, whether they are infants, middle schoolers, college bound – there is never a convenient time for kids to go through a divorce.

I don't know about you, but I don't want to sit back and let my child become a statistic. I remember very clearly thinking and praying, asking God to tell me what I could do to give my kids a fighting chance at being okay. What was revealed to my head and my heart was this:

I will love their father.

Before you throw the book across the room, give me a second. I know this isn't easy. Trust me. But you're not doing it for your ex-husband. You're doing it for your child, and your child is worth it.

However you feel about your husband receiving the prefix "ex," one thing remains true, he is still your child's father, and that fact carries an enormous weight. I believed as a wife and mother that part of my job was to help my husband be the best dad he could be. That hasn't changed just because we are no longer married, but it is definitely more difficult.

So how do you love him? What does this look like? Well, it looks a whole lot like this:

Love is patient, love is kind. It is not jealous, it is not pompous, it is not inflated, it is not rude, it does not seek its own interests, it is not quick-tempered, it does not brood over injury, it does not rejoice over wrongdoing but rejoices with the truth. It bears all things, believes all things, hopes all things, endures all things. Love never fails.

> Was that passage from 1 Corinthians read at your wedding? It really is a perfect guide for loving your spouse. The funny thing is, it's also the perfect guide for loving your ex-spouse.

Was that passage from 1 Corinthians read at your wedding? It really is a perfect guide for loving your spouse. The funny thing is, it's also the perfect guide for loving your ex-spouse.

Loving him means you have to be vulnerable. You have to bite your tongue. You have to put your pride on the back burner. It does *not* mean you have to be walked on. But you do have to approach moments of conflict with respect. What if he doesn't reciprocate? Do it anyway. It is easier to be angry, to shut everything else out, but I'll tell you what. That is exhausting.

Have you rolled your eyes so many times that you're dizzy? Are you arguing with me by saying I don't understand your situation, what *he's* like? You're right. I don't. But that still doesn't mean it's impossible. God understands your pain and frustration, and He wants to get you through this.

You will mess up. You will have moments where you're not being loving. But dust yourself off and try again. If you don't know where to start, start by praying for your ex-husband. This might be the most important thing you can do for your child's relationship with his father. If you can pray *with* your child for dad … go for it. Your kid will look back years down the road and say, "Man, my mom. She's got some character." If you don't want to pray for him, ask God to give you the desire. And if you are feeling particularly strong one day, ask for the ability to forgive and then cooperate with that grace. That is where the life-changing stuff happens.

It's my prayer that if your heart is hardened because you've been hurt and this is the chapter you like the least, this is where God will prove his power the most. He wants this for you and for your children. Whether they are three or thirty, he wants them to have more than a fighting chance. For each one of them, He wants a life of peace, love and, I'm fairly certain, a head with only two ears. Now brush off the book and apologize to it for throwing it across the room.

What Matters Most: To Do List

If you're still engaged in a civil war with your Ex, try some of these pointers:

- There are great classes on learning to co-parent in peace with your Ex taking one of those can give you some tips when things get difficult.

- Do you still harbor feelings of bitterness and anger towards your ex-husband? Go see a counselor and pray that God gives you peace.

- Next time you're tempted to say something negative about your ex-husband, bite your tongue. If he's made a mistake, the kids probably already know, and you have an opportunity for a character-building moment.

- Pray for your ex, but also pray for guidance in having a successful co-parent relationship. Sometimes just talking to God about it eases your stress.

- Read 1 Corinthians 13:4-8. If you don't have a bible, just look it up online. Use this as a guide for how to deal with the difficult waters of co-parenting. Remember how much you love your children and start there.

Chapter Eight

Don't Let the Mess Distract You

Shirley

My divorce created chaos in my life. I had to find a place to live, pay bills I wasn't sure I could afford, make decisions alone that I'd never had to make before. I found myself for many months living in a state of constant panic. It seemed like all I could do was worry and overthink and then worry and overthink some more.

At night, my mind would churn, and sleep became elusive and rare. That would create more stress for the next day, which would add to my panic. Some nights, I woke up in the middle of the night, heart racing, so worried about what the next day would bring.

For me, a person who absolutely hates limbo and holds tight to structure and predictability, all of that made my stress levels shoot higher every week. I couldn't control much of anything in my life right then. The harder I tried to control it, the worse things seemed to get.

I wasn't present in my life. I wasn't present for my friends or my family or my kids. I was caught in this endless loop of worry, and it was draining me of the experiences I wanted to have. I didn't know what to do.

It was my son, the no-schedule, let's-just-wing-it kid, who came to me and told me I needed to meditate. He'd been doing it for a while, and he said it really helped him reduce his stress and made him happier. I had noticed a change in him — a calming, I guess you'd call it — since he'd started meditating.

Still, it took him a long time to talk me into it. I thought it was crazy, New Age stuff. And besides, where was I going to find the time? My days were packed with workouts and work, and all those minutes I spent panicking about paying bills or meeting deadlines.

I don't know why I finally tried it. I think it was one of those days when the panic and stress had gotten so overwhelming I would have done anything to make those feelings stop. I went into my room, downloaded a how-to meditate video on YouTube, and for six minutes (no way was I ready for twenty minutes of meditation yet), I did nothing other than breathe.

I didn't work. I didn't clean. I didn't run errands. I didn't look at the clock or worry about the bills. I breathed, in and out, in and out, over and over again. For a long time, it felt stupid. It's just breathing, right? But then there was this moment, a split second, really, when my mind went –

Blank.

> It was a moment of quiet in my chaotic head so profound I started to cry. For a moment there, I truly let the rest of my worries go.

It was a moment of quiet in my chaotic head so profound I started to cry. For a moment there, I truly let the rest of my worries go. It was literally a second, but that was more than enough to convince me meditation was a good thing.

I have kept on meditating, ironically more often when things get scarier or busier. If I find time to meditate, everything on my plate becomes easier to bear. I find I am more present with those I love, and my mind is quiet so I can listen to what my friend is sharing or what my brother is worried about. My son meditates almost daily and spends a lot of his off-the-clock time taking walks in the woods or reading a book under the shade of a tree. He lives those hours with a loose abandon that I admire.

I watch him just … breathe, and I find myself doing the same. A calm washes over me, and I loosen my grip on my worries. I breathe in, I breathe out, and my mind makes room in the chaos for a little bit of sweet, wonderful peace.

Liza

Motherhood is a long journey, filled with many doubts and moments when you wonder if you're on the right path. If you're like me, or many of my mom friends, you have those quiet moments when you are alone and so many questions run through your mind. All of them come back to one core thought: What do my children really need?

Is it to excel in school? At sports? Achieving only A's? Or find their sense of self-esteem and belonging?

Don't Let the Mess Distract You

It could be yes to all the above, but when you really pare it down, what your children truly need is *you*. Your love, your presence, your dependability, you and all that you can be in their lives.

> I realized very early that they are watching how I move through this life, and drawing their own lessons from my decisions.

In the almost twelve years I have been blessed to be my daughters' mom, the girls' lives have changed, sometimes for the better, sometimes not, but throughout those times, they have looked to me for guidance on how to live through their experiences. I realized very early that they are watching how I move through this life, and drawing their own lessons from my decisions. Recently I have felt led to speak to my daughters about some sensitive topics like drugs and negative peer pressure. As I spoke about what it means to follow their friends in their friends' life decisions, I noticed a little bit of "yeah mom, we know ..." kind of discounting me as I spoke. This brought me back to reiterate to myself that it isn't what I say that matters, it is what I do, as in, it is "who I am" in this life as their example.

I used to have a mom friend who seemed to provide everything for her son. Anything he asked for, she bought. Any meal he requested, she made, regardless of what she had planned for dinner. Despite her best efforts to keep her son happy, he acted out often and frequently got into trouble. I listened to the mother explain it all away. I tried to listen in a nonjudgmental way and see each explanation for what it was.

To me, though, it all seemed to boil down to one thing – time.

Both his parents worked a crazy number of hours, and more often than not, they missed bedtimes and school mornings. Weekends were packed with errands and trips, and their son was often left with a sitter or relative. He had everything he wanted – except the thing he really wanted. Time with his parents.

According to Pew Research Center, on average, mothers spend 13.5 hours per week with their children and fathers spend 7.3 hours. Is this enough? Or is it not only the amount of time spent with children but the *quality* of the time spent that matters?

> If our children really need both time in their day to day living, and quality time to build those life lessons and memories, how do we change our parenting lives toward this goal?

If our children really need both time in their day to day living, and quality time to build those life lessons and memories, how do we change our parenting lives toward this goal?

First, reassess your weekly schedule. There will be some minutes, hours that you can find and reassign to quality time with your children. I've found using our drive time to and from school is a good moment for quality conversations, as well as prayer time with my children. I spend many of those moments simply listening to what is going on in their worlds.

Eating together, once an old-fashioned must, is coming back into popularity because it's a great way to get some face time with your kids. Even if I'm rushed and busy and know I could eat faster alone at the counter and get back to my To Do list, I make it a point to sit down with them at the table. I don't allow technology – no phones, iPads, television – because I want them to be present with each other and me, just as I am present with them. We might just be discussing swim team practice or their latest math or music test, but to kids, having a parent invested in their world is vital and shows them they are important, even in the small events.

At the baby shower for my first child, my father told me that one of the single most important gifts I could give my children was to fully listen to them. That lesson was lost on me in those early years after childbirth, until my oldest daughter started to talk. I remember getting down to her level. In the back of my mind, I was thinking of the hundreds of things I had to worry about and do. Then I stopped and shifted into the "active listening" I had learned in the workplace. I listened to her fully, acknowledged what she was saying, and repeated it back to her. The more I listened, the more she opened up, and the closer we got.

Now my daughters are ten and twelve, on the cusp of those interesting teenage years. I hope and pray that by laying that groundwork in all those car rides and dinners and moments on the playground, they will know that I am always there to fully listen and support them. And someday down the road, I will pull them aside when they have their own children and share the last and most important lesson – listen to your children, and remember you are who they aspire to be.

Abby

I remember the first load of baby laundry I ever did.

We received tons of clothes, all covered in boats, cars, blue plaid, argyle. Each piece was cuter than the last. I bought the Dreft detergent for sensitive baby skin and stood in front of the dryer while the load finished so I could take it out and fold it before it wrinkled.

I held up a pair of plaid shorts that had been fashioned out of maybe a quarter yard of fabric and my husband said, "I can't believe he is going to be so small!" The socks got to me. These tiny feet that were pressing into my ribs were soon going to be inside of them. The clothes were all so small and delicate.

And then I blinked.

Out with the newborn clothes. Then the 3 – 6 months. Before I knew it, he was in 2T and my baby was grown.

Writer Gretchen Rubin said, "The days are long but the years are short." As difficult as each 24-hour period is, with tantrums, loads of laundry, spilled drinks, and wet beds, it does feel like, collectively, they are flying by and I'm missing a lot of them.

Every mom worries about being (or not being) present to her children. As a single mom, the pressure is even greater because for many of us, our time with our kids is limited. The day I went to mediation for my divorce, I signed away Christmas morning with my boys in every odd-numbered year. I had to wrap my head around that. I only get nine out of eighteen Christmas mornings, so I'm going to take in every second.

Christmas is one thing, but how do we savor time and be fully present in the everyday, especially when every day can be daunting? I learned to take that cue from my parents, as I watched them become fabulous grandparents.

I think the reason grandparents have so much fun with kids is not only because, as the joke goes, they get to return them at the end of the day, but also because they've finally got the joy of parenting figured out.

One summer day, my mom popped in for a quick visit. When she arrived, we were playing in the front yard. It had rained a few hours earlier, so the shady parts of the yard were still a little wet.

We got our toys together and headed up the sidewalk. My mom said, "Look at those little feet!" I looked back, and one of my sons and I had left footprints on the sidewalk. His tiny prints were perfectly formed and perfectly cute. I thought to myself, "I never would've noticed them if she hadn't said something."

> ... I *do* think we need to take a break from being parental every now and again to see God's amazing work manifested in our little ones.

We don't always have a chance to "check out the footprints" or step back and take it all in. There is so much disciplining or cleaning up that needs to be done. I think that's ok. We can't be too hard on ourselves, but I *do* think we need to take a break from being parental every now and again to see God's amazing work manifested in our little ones.

The phrase, "being present" can be anxiety inducing. I know there are more times during the day when I am not present than when I am. So I'm going to *practice* presence just like one would practice the piano. I don't expect to be perfect, but

I expect to get better as I go on. There is so much beauty in those little moments, or footprints in this case. I don't know about you, but I have a feeling the foot that once fit in that tiny sock and left that little print on the sidewalk will be as big as mine before I know it.

What Matters Most: To Do List

If you are having a tough time being present, try our tips below:

- Practice being present by looking at something in your child that they will eventually grow out of like chubby hands, sweet pigtails, or awkward stubble.

- Try meditation. There are several great free intro videos on YouTube and a couple of free apps (Meditation Studio has different meditations for different moments, like anxiety or anger or sleep).

- Focus on paying complete attention to whomever you are talking with. Whenever you feel your mind wander, bring it right back to that person. They will notice, and

- Prayer can be another form of meditation. When things are overwhelming or you feel like you are losing your grasp on what's important, take a moment to pray. Tony Robbins says that gratitude and stress can't exist in the same space, so start with expressing gratitude.

- Call your parents or an older relative and ask them what part of parenting they miss the most. When you are experiencing those same moments, make a more concerted effort to be present, to hold on to those memories.

- Next time you're tempted to take your phone out and snap a picture, just take a deep breath and capture the moment in your memory.

Chapter Nine
Thank You is More Than Good Manners

Shirley

Gratitude.

The older I get, the more I realize how important it is. I have seen the shows that advise you to write down three things each day that you are grateful for, and for a while, I did that. Then I found I was putting the same things down every day – my kids, the roof over my head, and the money in my bank account – and I realized it wasn't really gratitude if it had become rote.

My new approach to gratitude came about at the same time I made the change to be more compassionate, more present, and calmer. I started meditating and reading books that fostered that attitude of compassion and presence. And in the process, I came across a lot of advice about being grateful.

Now when my heart is heavy, I take a walk. I leave my phone behind, and I concentrate on the tiniest things I am grateful for – the whisper of the breeze through the leaves on the trees, the shells that line the shore's edge, the birds that dart in and out of the incoming tide. I remember walking through my neighborhood at dusk and looking up at the trees. The blue-purple light coming through the branches was touched with a bit of fog, and it all seemed so magical and precious and beautiful. I thanked God for that moment of beauty, for that calm in a busy day.

I have started practicing gratitude with the people in my life, too. I try to send more thank-you cards. Try to say thank you more often. I leave notes in my son's lunch — even though he is eighteen and taking that lunch to a job — that tell him how grateful I am that he's a great kid. I send my daughter cards that say the same thing.

My Calendar is Written in Crayon

> If you really think about it and become more conscious of those tiny moments, gratitude becomes a way of life.

Throughout the day, I try to say thank you to God as often as I can. Thank you for helping me arrive at my destination safely. Thank you for taming my tongue when I wanted to say something unkind. Thank you for a wonderful memory with a friend. If you really think about it and become more conscious of those tiny moments, gratitude becomes a way of life. I've noticed my son has become more grateful with the people around him, more at peace. I'd like to think he's picking up a little of that from watching me.

I mentioned earlier that Tony Robbins says gratitude and stress can't coexist. That when your stress gets out of control, focus on gratitude. He's right. The more I do that, the smaller my problems become. They're still there, but they feel manageable.

I am grateful for that advice — not for the problems, but for the fact that what seemed like a mountain now appears as a hill I am fully capable of climbing. I don't need to make a list at the end of the day because I am looking for those moments all the time. And the funny thing is, the more often I am grateful, the easier it becomes to find things to thank God for.

So take a moment today to leave your phone behind, step outside, and look up. Admire the trees, the birds, the sun in the sky. Bend down to the grass and be grateful for the ecosystem that keeps the world moving. Gratitude blooms in those moments and fills your heart, nudging out the bitterness and stress. And that is something to truly be grateful for.

Liza

I have been very fortunate in my life. Maybe that is why I have always lived my life with gratitude. I grew up knowing three of my four grandparents, which meant they were present in my life, sharing their histories and their wisdom, and providing a guiding hand when I needed one. They were some of my best cheerleaders and brought another level of kindness and love to my life that I miss to this day, decades after they have all passed away.

I've also been blessed to have the positive influence from other strong women in my life, my Godmother Gloria, and three of my aunties.

Their influence, and my parents', made me a positive thinking person. At work, I'm the one who

My Calendar is Written in Crayon

limits complaints and focuses on remaining positive. This helps breed positivity through the whole workplace, like a healthy set of dominoes.

When something very tragic happened in my life at age 39, I think it was the first time I ever experienced true, deep sadness. I remember saying to my close friends that I've always felt grateful to have the amazing life I have had for nearly four decades. Even with that one tough period, I truly feel that I have lived a life that is nothing less than blessed, and for this I am grateful.

> That's the spirit I want to give to my daughters. I want gratefulness to play an important role in our lives.

That's the spirit I want to give to my daughters. I want gratefulness to play an important role in our lives.

Sometimes I'll look in the rearview mirror while I'm driving my daughters to school or practice and notice their two dark-haired heads together, deep in a conversation filled with genuine laughter and joy. I take a moment then to say "Thank you, Jesus" for keeping these girls so close in sisterly love. That extends into other areas of our lives – Julia helping Olivia with her homework sometimes or Olivia picking up Julia's dishes from the table just to be kind.

If my daughters grow up with grateful hearts, experiencing a daily life full of gratitude, I am confident they will never look at themselves as entitled. Hopefully, they will become kindhearted, humble, and grateful adults and spread that attitude of gratitude everywhere they go. When you live your life with gratitude, you are able to see the amazing and abundant blessings in front of you and all around you

For many years, I had a life of financial abundance, but learned very quickly that money doesn't make people happy. The lifestyle of having money brings can be amazing. However, when you come home from these vacations or shopping trips, you also come home to your own unhappiness.

So I have learned to focus on those things I am grateful for. In no particular order, here is the list I hold in my heart:

1. My daughters behaving like best friends

2. A job that doesn't require working on the weekends away from them

3. A close set of friends who are centered in Christ

4. A school that teaches my children about His ways

5. Living in an incredibly sunny place

6. His grace in all I do

7. Snuggles in the early morning with my daughters

8. Gas in my car and food in our refrigerator

9. Our energetic and loving church

10. Our God

I know, without a doubt, if you don't look at your life with eyes full of gratefulness, you will never find your happiness. Of this, I'm sure. Start with gratitude, and all the rest will fall into place.

Abby

My freshman year of college I lived in a dorm. Not a fancy dorm with apartment-style living. No, I'm talking tiny room with a view of the dumpster, a kitchen that never has a clean sink, and gang bathrooms type of dorm. One of the crummy parts of dorm life was the constant need to wear shoes. Even in our own little space that we kept clean, my roommate and I always wore flip flops, and we wouldn't dream of walking down the hall or taking a shower without them. No way.

When I went home for Thanksgiving that year, it was my first time home since the semester began. I got in the shower at my parents' house and nearly cried. I could feel the porcelain on the bottoms of my feet! I hadn't felt that in nearly three months, and I missed it

> It's difficult to be mindful of the blessings around us because so many of them are just part of everyday life.

Before that moment, if you had told me that a simple shower floor would make me tear up, I would've looked at you like you were crazy.

It's difficult to be mindful of the blessings around us because so many of them are just part of

My Calendar is Written in Crayon

everyday life. Having a job (even if it's not one we are passionate about), a toothbrush, working tires on the car, a vegetable with dinner. The list is endless.

As a single mom, the blessings are still there, but there are so many "to do's" in each day that gratitude falls way down the list of priorities. We might even find ourselves saying, "Things are so hard. I feel like I have nothing to be grateful for." When we are struggling to pay the bills on time and another note comes home from school asking for $5 toward a gift for the art teacher, we can forget to be grateful for the good school our kids attend. When we're up in the middle of the night running with a bowl to the bedside, we can forget to appreciate the warm bed they have to sleep in when the flu hits. And when work asks us to stay late to help meet a deadline, it's easy to forget that we are a valued member of the team.

We might not even notice that a blessing in disguise was in the works. For me, that came in the form of baby carrots and chicken nuggets. I volunteered to bring the carrots to my sons' preschool Thanksgiving potluck. I bought enough baby carrots to feed a small army of preschoolers, and two days later received the menu assigning me chicken nuggets. I was upset, not only because I had already bought the stinkin' carrots, but also because I felt like no one appreciated I was a single mom. Why did I need to bring one of the most expensive things? Someone else got to dump four cans of corn into a bowl, and I have to purchase and bake nuggets?

As I was whining to a friend about the potluck assignment, I realized that earlier that month I had been given a gift card for Chick-fil-A that included a free small nugget platter. I had to chuckle because I had been too busy thinking of myself to notice how God was actually blessing me. With the gift card, I could get something for free with no cooking required!

Showing gratitude is something that takes practice, so I have been trying to speak it aloud. Too often we *think* of a compliment or gratitude, but we don't verbalize it. Now when I'm with my kids, I'll say, "You give the best hugs" or "This ice cream is really tasty." I hope I'm teaching them there are blessings all around us. Even when life is tough, if we zoom out and change our perspective, we will see them. And just maybe if I practice gratitude with them enough, they'll have it down pat before they're wearing flip flops in the shower.

What Matters Most: To Do List

If you are having trouble finding your gratitude, try these tips:

- Next time you realize you are thankful for something, say it aloud. Say it to your children, God, your boss, even the guy in the Starbucks line!

- Take a moment to unplug and just notice the small things around you, and be grateful for them.

- Try to turn stresses into moments of gratitude. Running late for a meeting? Be grateful for the extra time you spent getting your child ready for school. Out of an ingredient for dinner? Be grateful for the opportunity to show your kids you can be creative. Talked to a friend until the wee hours of a morning and now you're dragging at work? Be grateful you could be a rock for someone who needed one.

- Start a gratitude journal or keep a post-it pad in your purse. Every time you think of something to be grateful for, write it down.

✏ Write down the top ten things you are grateful for. The next week, write another, new ten, and so on.

Chapter Ten

What Matters Most of All

Shirley

Just before I got divorced, I spent three days on the floor of my living room, sorting through the boxes and boxes of pictures and photo albums we had accumulated over the years. I divided them into four piles – one for each of my kids, one for my ex, and one for me. Like many people, I had plenty of double prints to spread out among everyone.

It was all so bittersweet, sifting through two decades of memories and divvying them up into little piles. There was my daughter as a newborn, then later as a toddler, her favorite bear under her arm and her thumb in her mouth. My son the constant eater, asleep in his high chair with his face

in a bowl of spaghetti. There were visits with Santa, trips to the park, encounters with hungry goats at the zoo. Then, the later years with school concerts, proms, and graduations.

Every snapshot captured one moment in time, a moment that seemed to last forever when I was living it, but now, looking back, was gone in a blink. How I wished I could go back and relive those moments and pay more attention, imprinting every last toothy smile on my brain.

> Despite the ups and downs, we had created a lot of pretty awesome memories in those years, and I wished I could hold tight to every last one.

I remember crying a lot during those days with regret, with happiness, with a crazy mixture of emotions. Despite the ups and downs, we had created a lot of pretty awesome memories in those years, and I wished I could hold tight to every last one.

My grandmother was one of those people who remembered every person she ever met, every street she lived on, the directions to every house she owned. I once asked her how she knew all those things still, even though she was well into her nineties. She said, "I have a lot of time to sit here and think. So I go back to each memory and think about it until I have all the details in my head again. I remember those days, over and over again, and it's like I'm still there."

My Calendar is Written in Crayon

I've tried to do that more with my kids in the last couple of years. We have a lot of "remember when" conversations, and I've shared a lot more about my childhood with them. My kids are adults now, so we can have those kinds of late into the night conversations that I hope they will remember when they have their own children.

I have a digital photo frame that used to run the same hundred or so pictures every single day. I've started changing that up, adding new photos to greet me when I walk in the door, so that it triggers other memories and special moments. Maybe I'm just getting sentimental as I get older, but I think doing that helps me do what my grandmother did – sit and think until the memory that was a little foggy and hard to grasp has come back as clear and strong and real as the day it happened.

It's those little moments, I believe, that matter the most. Those lazy afternoons when one of the babies would fall asleep on my chest, and I'd hold so very still, wanting to remember those hours forever. The feel of my nervous daughter's hand in mine on her first day of preschool, the sound of my son exclaiming "Mom!" when he saw me in the parking lot at the end of the school day. The times my teenager left me a note because I had a rough morning, or my adult daughter sat beside me in the kitchen, learning how to make pies on Thanksgiving morning.

Those are the moments I remember with my own parents, the memories I cling to when I miss my late mom so very much. They're the kind of memories I hold in that space between me and my children as they grow up and away and move onto the next phase of their lives. And someday down the road, when they are grown and settled, I hope those memories become the threads that knit our hearts together.

Liza

My youngest daughter loves to wear makeup and transform herself into everything from a ballerina to a princess. For the last three Christmases, she has asked Santa for a makeup kit. She'll put on her dance shoes and beg me to watch yet another home performance.

Sometimes I'll be in the middle of cooking dinner, finishing a proposal, or just plain tired. I'd love to say I always stopped and watched her, but honestly I did not. Many times I would only half-watch, not

My Calendar is Written in Crayon

focused on her request of me but enveloped in my own multi-tasking, schedule-crazed day.

Those are the days that test me, as a mother, as a person. I've been a business owner, completely 100% responsible for each and every part of my business, for nearly twenty years. I have found it's easy to work together as a team when the road is smooth. It's when the road is difficult that the real work begins, and we really have to find out how to get along and still build an amazing company.

I think this is what parenting is like. It is easy to stay ahead of all things with your kids when the ride is easy. When the money isn't an issue, when the grades are great, when you have support around you *and* when you are feeling great about yourself. Not to mention, an easy schedule, lots of free time, and a short To Do list. Those are the weekends when I give praise and thanks to God abundantly and take my daughters on a weekend excursion. Life is bright and pretty and seems perfect.

But on the days when dinner isn't easily made, debt collectors are calling and your bank account is at a near-zero balance, or the kids are fighting, that's when it matters most that you keep your cool, find your strength, and keep focused on taking the very best care of your children.

For me, that's not just about cooking healthy meals or enforcing bedtimes. It's about setting an example for living life, rather than spending my days lecturing or correcting my children. I want to live the kind of life I want my daughters to emulate. In the end, it won't be the accolades I may have achieved while operating my business or serving in the community, it will be the fact they have seen me day in and day out, modeling how to handle life's challenges as a strong and courageous, faith-led woman.

I am acutely aware that my daughters repeat the words I say and their behavior is sometimes an exact imitation of my own. They treat people with respect or less than the proper respect by watching my interactions. For me, there is no question the life I lead will influence them greatly in their lives. The bible verse, **For me and my household, we shall serve the Lord,** is a verse I stand strong on as I believe the "serving" Him encompasses all areas of our lives.

Because of the strength I have found in Him, I want my daughters to have a fully encompassing relationship with Jesus along with a stellar education. I know in the end this will benefit their lives greatly and they will become the people they were meant to me. But when I ask my daughters what they want, the answer is more roundabout.

A hoverboard, says the youngest. The latest books in a favorite series, says the oldest. But if I listen long enough, I'll hear them both say the same thing – they want time. Time with me, time with their father who lives far away. Our children want our time and to see our efforts to make time in their life for what they value most.

So the daily challenge is how to provide this time for them to enjoy what they are passionate about. Sound familiar? Most of us point to this as our daily goal. The problem is that we can sometimes find more reasons why this can't happen than ways to make it work with our children.

In my house, we rarely have Saturday activities. I don't make commitments outside of church on

Sundays. The activities my girls are involved in are very close in proximity to our household. This is the way I find what I term as their "down time" and they think of as "play time."

But it's about more than hours. It's about presence. I am my daughters' number-one cheerleader and the one human being in this world they can count unconditionally. When I was young, my mother and father were my number-one cheerleaders. My father was the one with a ready voice of reason or a bit of wisdom. Sadly, I have met people who don't have a single human being they can depend on 100% of the time, nor do they have anyone that they believe loves them with 100% unconditional love.

As my girls go through their lives, transform from children to adults and someday to parents of their own, I hope they will be able to draw on all those moments we had together and all those lessons that were solidified in my actions. That they will no matter where they are, how far they go or how old they get, understand I will always love them and always believe in them.

My Calendar is Written in Crayon

Abby

For nine chapters, Shirley, Liza, and I have attempted to share how we are navigating life as single, working moms. Is it the blind leading the blind? In a lot of ways, yeah, because life is rarely static. From year to year, kids grow, work dynamics change, and people come into and go out of our lives.

So what matters most? What never changes and can always be relied upon?

Ice cream and wine.

Okay, maybe that's a chapter in another book.

> ... what matters most to me is love. That is what carries us over every hurdle and through every trial. It accompanies us in every celebration and every milestone like an invaluable friend just waiting to be invited over.

Seriously, what matters most to me is love. That is what carries us over every hurdle and through every trial. It accompanies us in every celebration and every milestone like an invaluable friend just waiting to be invited over.

What Matters Most of All

Does love seem like an obvious answer? Like you were looking to crack the code on the lock only to find out it's 1,2,3,4,5? It's powerful, yet we ignore its importance because of its simplicity. Like a good chef will recognize that plain old salt is the most important ingredient in his pantry, a smart and savvy single, working mom knows love is all. She also knows that just like in marriage, love is not just an emotion, it's a decision and an action.

When my divorce became imminent, I resolved to lead my life with love. I would lead the divorce proceedings with love, lead my interactions with my ex-husband with love, and lead my children with love. I'd seen too many people get eaten from the inside out by anger, resentment, and fear, and I knew I couldn't survive like that.

In what I consider a miracle, on a day that I had forgotten that resolution to love, God showed me that anger was not the way. During my marriage, I rarely spoke up for myself or voiced what I wanted; I was a doormat of sorts. So on this occasion when my ex-husband violated the trust we established as co-parents, I felt justified in losing my temper. I drove to his apartment, looking for a knock-down, drag-out fight only to find him not there. I called several times, and when he finally picked up the phone, I pulled my car into a parking spot in his apartment complex and yelled at the ceiling of my car, straining to get as close as I possibly could get to the Bluetooth microphone. I had never yelled like that before. I used words I had never said before. When the conversation was over, I hung up and felt like I had just punched Mike Tyson in the jaw and made him stagger. Turns out some damage had been done, not to my ex, but to myself.

For the next several months, out of the blue, I would lose my voice. The scratchiness sounded pretty cool at times, but as a radio host, this was a problem. I even had a listener call and tell me that she had to change the station when I did that with my voice because it bothered her, as if I had some control over it.

I finally went to an Ear, Nose, and Throat doctor and was diagnosed with a hematoma on one of my vocal cords. It was the result of a hemorrhaged blood vessel that was leaking blood into the cord tissue. If I didn't get it taken care of, there was potential I would have permanent damage and lose my voice all together.

He asked me if I had done any strenuous singing or yelling, and I thought back to the first time my voice went hoarse – the day I punched Mike Tyson. At the end of that conversation, my voice went out. I remember thinking it was odd because I never lost my voice, but figured it was because I had been crying.

The doctor told me I needed vocal rest. I laughed out loud, explaining I had two toddlers and a radio show – the opposite of silence! But we tried. It helped, but not enough. I needed surgery. So in June of 2015, I had surgery to remove the hematoma on my vocal cord and was not allowed to speak for two weeks.

Silence gives you a great deal of time to think. During those two weeks, God showed me that anger was not going to make me a better mom, nor was it going to make me effective in my job in radio ministry. In fact, he took away my ability to do *both* in order to reveal that to me. The lesson was so clear I couldn't ignore it. Anger would lead to death. Love would lead to life. So I chose love.

Maybe it's more complex than that. Maybe when work is grueling and the kids bring home a D in Science or say they want to go live with dad because he lets them stay up late, love doesn't feel like enough of a solution. But it's what matters most, and if you chose love, I think you'll always crack the code.

What Matters Most: To Do List

To find what matters most of all, try our suggestions:

- ✏ Know your end goal with your parenting and try to direct everything toward that.

- ✏ Know that this time in your life as an active, daily parent will pass by quickly and try to enjoy these days so you don't regret it later.

- ✏ Take a moment at the end of the day to write down one or two special moments with your kids. When they are grown and memories have faded, it will be a great way to relive those times.

- ✏ Think about an area of your life that needs more love, compassion, and mercy and less anger and bitterness. Make a concerted effort to be the source of that love through kind words, forgiveness, and grace.

- ✏ Get that journal out again and write down the three things that matter most to you in your life as a single, working mom. Maybe you've never asked yourself what matters the most to you. Here's an opportunity to put it on paper and start working toward making those things a priority.

- ✏ Spend more time in silence. There is so much noise and so many other people telling us what should matter most. Turning it all off for a few minutes a day will help us listen to ourselves and listen to what calms you.

About the Authors

Shirley Jump

Mom of two kids, an 18-year-old son and a 23-year-old daughter.

When she's not writing books, *New York Times* and *USA Today* bestselling author Shirley Jump competes in triathlons, mostly because all that training lets her justify mid-day naps and a second slice of chocolate cake. She's published more than 60 books in 24 languages, although she's too geographically challenged to find any of those countries on a map. Visit her website at www.ShirleyJump.com for author news and a booklist, and follow her on Facebook at www.Facebook.com/shirleyjump.author for give aways and deep discussions about important things like chocolate and shoes.

"Let the morning bring me word of your unfailing love, for I have put my trust in you. Show me the way I should go, for to you I entrust my life."

– Psalm 143: 8

To contact the author:

    Shirley@shirleyjump.com

    www.ShirleyJump.com

    @shirleyjump

About the Authors

Liza Marie Garcia

Mom of two daughters, ages 10 and 12.

This C-level executive mom has supported her employees, her former husband and her children fully with the technology company she founded in Seattle for more than fifteen years. She is now an Equity Partner in the Publishing and Promotion House of NOW SC Press. This is her second published book, after *Never Drink Coffee During a Business Meeting debuted in March of 2016*. She has completed a nationwide book signing tour for Barnes and Noble and speaks regularly to business professionals. She is dedicated completely to her ten- and twelve-year-old daughters and believes Jesus is the Head of her household.

About the Authors

"For I know the plans I have for you, declares the Lord, plans to prosper and not to harm you, plans to give you hope and a future."

– Jeremiah 29:11

To contact the author:

Liza@lizamariegarcia.com

Facebook: Liza Marie Garcia (Byrne)

@lizagarciaceo

Abby Brundage

Mom of two sons, ages 3 and 5.

There are 24 hours in the day and (most days) Abby strives to use those hours to come to know, love and serve God in a deeper way. She'll tell you her marriage, divorce and children have been huge in helping her achieve that. She's the mom of two sweet and savory little boys who can't decide from day to day if they are Storm Troopers, priests or fire fighters. Abby is the host of *The Big Big House Morning Show* on WBVM/Spirit FM 90.5. She loves music that makes her head bob, hearing listeners' stories and getting to share her life with them.

> "Perhaps this is the moment for which you have been created."
>
> – Esther 4:14

About the Authors

To contact the author:

> Abby.brundage@gmail.com
>
> www.abbybrundage.com
>
> @abbyspirit

Look for our next What Matters Most of All books!

Buy What Matters Most of All: There's a Fish in the Clothes Dryer by Francis Fernandez online at http://www.nowscpress.com/fish in March 2017.

#WMMFish

Look for Shirley Jump's latest great book!

Buy The Perfect Recipe for Love and Friendship by Shirley Jump online and in stores everywhere, July 2017.

A Day in the Life

Shirley

My alarm always goes off way too early, and almost always at a time with a four at the beginning of it. I work out before the sun rises (since I live in Florida and it gets crazy hot after sunrise), and do my workouts with friends. Honestly, ninety percent of the reason I get out of bed at all is because I know they're waiting for me and I don't want to be the lazy one who didn't show up.

My kids are adults now. My twenty three year old lives on her own, and my eighteen year old lives with me. He's responsible enough to get up in the morning without my nagging, so I don't have to worry too much if my workout goes late. I still make him breakfast and lunch most days, and still tuck in a note once in a while, just because.

There's a certain freedom that comes with kids being adults. I noticed in my triathlons that the heaviest concentration of women competitors is in that forty- to fifty-year old range. Most of us at that age have grown children, or at least kids who can be left home alone, so we finally have time to pick up running or cycling or whatever hobby we have put off all those years.

I work at home, so my day is usually spent on the sofa, writing. My son gets home around four, and nine times out of ten, has plans with his friends. On the rare nights when he doesn't, he and I will either go out for a quick bite or I'll make something. He still really likes homemade dinners – and the leftovers for lunch the next day.

I think back to how my days used to be, with toddlers and running to school and soccer practices, and never quite feeling like I was caught up. My life was hectic but full, and at the end of the day, when I'd peek in on my sleeping children, I'd take a moment to count my blessings.

I still do that, when my son stops to give me a hug or my daughter calls just to say she loves me. Those are the times that make all those long ago crazy days worth it. Then I go back to my present quiet day with a smile.

But if you pressed me, I'd admit that I miss those days when the kids were young. I miss the noise and

My Calendar is Written in Crayon

the laughs and most of all, the snuggles before bedtime. Now I hold those memories in my heart — and dream of grandchildren.

My Calendar is Written in Crayon

Will you share your ...

"Day In The Life?"

Go to www.nowscpress.com/DITL

- Enter your Day to share with our mom community
- Enter to win a Starbucks card

One $10 Starbucks card per month.

Your entry stays eligible for the length of the contest.

Because we think every mom deserves a free cup of coffee every once in a while!

#SCWLife #WMMCrayon

A Day in the Life

Liza

It was the day before Valentine's Day, and it got off to a rough start. My ten year old wanted to stay home, insisting she was still sick, even after missing three days of school last week. I reminded her that she'd been healthy enough to partake in all of her big sister's twelfth birthday activities this past weekend. Turns out my youngest daughter was struggling with getting back into the wakeup routine, and hadn't finished all of her homework.

That debate made our morning rushed. Instead of leaving by 7:10, as we usually do on Mondays (so my eldest can be on the school's radio morning show), we ended up being late and missing the radio show.

The day just got more rushed from there, as most days tend to be. I dropped the girls off, took a conference call with our new graphic artist in the car, on my way to a business meeting with a new magazine contributor. Rush from that meeting to another one across town. In between, I drank tons of coffee and green tea to keep my energy up.

I missed lunch, then hurried to the girls' school at the end of the day. I was late there, too, and they were already calling, asking when I would be there.

We duck into the grocery store on the way to swim team practice to buy the Valentine's cards and candy the girls need for school tomorrow. I finally take a bit of a breath while the girls are at practice, and spend that hour and a half returning emails and trying to check off at least one item on Monday's to do list.

I make a quick and easy dinner of pasta, and we have a few minutes to catch up as a family before I run my younger daughter to dance class at 7:15 p.m., and leave the eldest home to finish her homework.

 I have another hour to return emails and get some work done as I wait outside the dance studio.

By nine, both the girls are in bed, and I find myself with a quiet house, an ice water at my bedside and my laptop, iPad, and phone surrounding me. I finally have uninterrupted time to work. But instead of feeling stressed or frustrated, I take a moment to pray.

"Thank you God," I whisper, "for a day filled with my daughters' amazing lives!" I am incredibly grateful to be their mom!

My Calendar is Written in Crayon

Will you share your ...

"Day In The Life?"

Go to www.nowscpress.com/DITL

- Enter your Day to share with our mom community
- Enter to win a Starbucks card

One $10 Starbucks card per month.

Your entry stays eligible for the length of the contest.

Because we think every mom deserves a free cup of coffee every once in a while!

#SCWLife #WMMCrayon

Abby

My day usually starts before my alarm even goes off, thanks to my three year old who rarely sleeps through the night. Thankfully, this particular morning, he comes in my room instead of calling out for me to come to him.

The big morning emergency? He wanted to tell me that his pajama pants were green. I mumbled something like "that's cool, bud," and told him to go back to bed. He asked for one more kiss and one more hug and then told me he loved me. Any irritation I felt at being woken up at three in the morning disappeared with his sweetness. I'm in trouble with this one.

My alarm goes off at 4:20 a.m. and I get ready as quietly as a mouse in a house full of underfed, sleeping cats. I wait to put my shoes on until I'm in the garage, so as not wake my sleeping boys. Before I head out to the driveway to meet up with the sitter just after five, I spend ten minutes reading a few pages of a book and praying. God must hear some crazy prayers from me then because this is all pre-caffeine!

From six to ten in the morning I push buttons and play music on the radio. I know my parents tune in every day, so there are at least two people listening. My co-host and I attempt to inspire, encourage and entertain. Sometimes we pull it off and sometimes we flop, but it's always a good time. Today we shared about our favorite romantic comedy. Anytime I get to quote "When Harry Met Sally" it's a good day.

After work, my day looks like this:

Bribe my boys to take a nap. Lose that battle. Fight with light sabers. Make a snack. Build and protect Lego creations. Check to see if the betta fish is still alive. Sigh because it is and a double sigh because I need to clean his fishbowl and find the missing can of fish food. Make another snack. Drag my kids to the grocery store and try to convince them that the regular cart is just as cool as the racecar one (that is impossible to steer!).

By the time dinner, bath and stories roll around, I'd be just fine if my preschoolers tucked me in. I give "one more kiss and one more hug" about five times and then I finally head to bed to start everything all over again in a few hours. I'm tired, but I wouldn't

My Calendar is Written in Crayon

change a thing. Except for the fish. I'd be okay if it died.

My Calendar is Written in Crayon

Will you share your ...

"Day In The Life?"

Go to www.nowscpress.com/DITL

- Enter your Day to share with our mom community
- Enter to win a Starbucks card

One $10 Starbucks card per month.

Your entry stays eligible for the length of the contest.

Because we think every mom deserves a free cup of coffee every once in a while!

#SCWLife #WMMCrayon